Make More from Property

From investor thinking to a business mindset

— VICKI WUSCHE —

Make More Money from Property:
From investor thinking to a business mindset
Copyright ©2012 Vicki Wusche
Published in 2012 by SRA Books

SRA Books
Sue Richardson Associates
Minerva Mill Innovation Centre
Station Road
Alcester
Warwickshire B49 5ET
T: 01789 761345
www.suerichardson.co.uk

A CIP record for this book is available from the British Library.

ISBN 978-0-9567553-4-6

Designed, produced and published by Sue Richardson Associates.

Printed and bound in Great Britain by TJ International, Padstow, Cornwall

Make More Money from Property: From investor thinking to a business mindset is a breath of fresh air. It is honest and truthful about what it takes to be a success in your finances. Vicki understands that it takes more than just information; it also requires a knowledge of how to implement the actions that will bring success. This book deals with the whole and not just a slice of what it takes to make it in property investing and, to some degree, life. Highly recommended.

Denzil Edmeade www.gen-hope.co.uk

I discovered property investing at the end of 2009 and the following year jumped in with my wife Jane, buying 10 properties in 12 months. I met Vicki at many events during 2010 – she usually had a captivated audience listening to her pearls of wisdom so it was difficult to get close. We eventually had a long chat about many things property related, families and scuba diving. Around this time I subscribed to Vicki's sharp and insightful newsletters to get to know her better.

Vicki's first book, *Using Other People's Money*, was extremely relevant for me – at that time I had depleted funds and no confidence to approach investors. Why would they want to invest with me? I was trying to buy a large HMO and needed JV funding fast – a week later I had raised £75k from two sources. In 2011 when my son and daughter joined us, we switched our focus totally to multi-let properties, primarily for the enormous cash flow they give. I consider *Using Other People's Money* to be a manual, containing essential information for every property investor. I have since raised over £300k of other people's money and now have a definite system to follow whenever I need more funds.

What next? How do I change from a busy landlord into a business owner? Vicki's new book once again (spookily) arrived at just the right time. *Make More Money from Property* encourages you to examine your strategies, your portfolio and, most importantly, yourself. Vicki encourages the strategic development of your business – working on it not in it – alongside a solid life philosophy and core values. Subjects I had previously struggled with are clearly explained. I love the personable detail and the analogies. I got the feeling that if she could, Vicki would reach out of the book and give me a shake – 'Francis! Take action! More leverage!' This book will now take the place of *Using Other People's Money* in my man-bag! Before you start reading, grab a pen and paper! It's time to grow up and move on with your business with this coming-of-age professional property investor's book. Happy investing!

Francis Dolley – www.yourlocalinvestment.com "

Having had several property strategy sessions with Vicki over the last nine months, I had a really good understanding of what my property plans were from her guidance and expertise. Her second book really clarified the advice and has given me an on-going detailed reference point as my property business portfolio grows. I would recommend this book full of gems to even the most experienced investor.

Clare Gillbanks www.the-property-angel.co.uk

I have known Vicki since 2007 when she joined the special community we created called Ecademy. My first experience was a lovely walk on the Surrey Downs when we talked about love, family and life. At that moment I knew that this was a lady of principle, passion and power. Since that walk I have watched Vicki develop her business, constantly refining and defining, seeking the most perfect solution for her clients. Through creating workshops, webinars, training courses and now this fabulous book, I have seen her passionately pour herself into everything she does with the intention of providing access to her passion and knowledge at the flexible price points that people can afford in order to change their lives.

This book summarises everything that she has learned and experienced in business, much of which is applicable to any business arena and of course in particular property investment. I am sure that whether the reader is experienced or new to investing they will find many insights that will enable them to make a sound decision on the way they will invest their money for the future.

Penny Power, Co-Founder of Ecademy and Founder of Digital Youth Academy

I first met Vicki in 2007 when she joined Ecademy. At the time she said she was a business consultant although she admitted that she was not invoicing and so was really an unemployed consultant! When we talked at length recently I could see the clarity she has developed around her business and her brand. This book distils her learning over the last 2–3 years while she has built her property portfolio and financial security. It is a great read, easy and humorous, I recommend it to new investors and those more experienced as there are valuable tips for all.

Thomas Power, Co-Founder of Ecademy www.ecademy.com

The most relevant, passionate and strategy intensive book any property investor in the UK market can hope to buy. We were mesmerised by the impactful clarity and depth. A gift of time, money and advanced knowledge from the best exponent of expertise that mere mortals can emulate. Steve and Helen Green formerly known as the Stealth Millionaires until we read this book.

Steve and Helen Green

In these turbulent times, there are some words you don't often see in the same sentence – for example, money, finance, debt, intelligence, ethics and foresight. Vicki Wusche brings a breathe of fresh air to a subject many find either dull or inaccessible. This book explains money is an energy and a malleable force we can use for higher purpose and benefit. It is an essential read for investors of all types and those who would like to play but don't know where or how to start.

Tom Evans, author of *Flavours of Thought*

When it comes to property Vicki simply knows her stuff! Having worked from the ground up and having built her property portfolio from nothing, she not only understands the strategies required to build an extensive property portfolio, but also the mindset. Vicki actually gets out there and makes things happen – there is no theoretical advice in this book, only the real deal. If you want someone who is going to tell you what it really takes to get out there and Make Money from Property, who is actually doing it and has hands on experience and a wealth of knowledge, then Vicki is the real deal.

Johnnie Cass www.johnniecass.com

This is a well structured, informative and clear guide to property investing and sourcing as a business. I had no trouble reading the entire book in two sittings. It does exactly as it says on the tin – gives helpful tips, examples, data and facts on how to make wise property investment decisions for achieving a financially free life and how the knowledge we already have can become the stepping stone to a new stream of income through sourcing. The additional reading material Vicki recommends to her readers is highly relevant.

There is much humour in the book, which makes the subject matter less dry than many of the other property guides I have read. I particularly liked Vicki's colourful descriptions of estate agents and her observations concerning new species of mould in those stinky houses we are encouraged to view. Like the old adage 'where there's muck, there's brass', Vicki's strategies are spot on for finding good value properties with high rental yield. From the outset, the reader is encouraged to take active responsibility for achieving the wealth obtainable through property, to focus on the opportunities available and apply fresh thinking, eg. considering commercial lending rather than buy-to-let mortgages. *Make More Money from Property* comes highly recommended.

Lorraine Stylianou www.frida-kahlo.co.uk

Testimonials for *Using Other People's Money – How to Invest in Property*

I met Vicki in 2007 and it was hard not to get caught up in her enthusiasm for property. Vicki and I worked together on various training and development contracts over the next few years while she built her property portfolio. I was inspired and enthused by her resilience and focus. I didn't at that time think I could do it myself. I could, however, encourage, support and help Vicki celebrate her successes.

When Vicki wrote *Using Other People's Money* I immediately started reading. As I read it, flashes of insight and opportunity came my way and by the end of the book I knew how I could invest in property. I quickly took action, approached a family member with a win–win opportunity for us both and now we have our own portfolio!

To buy a copy of
Using Other People's Money
visit http://bit.ly/OPM-Book1

I have learnt so much about property from Vicki, who has an immense and in-depth knowledge. This means that I now have a 5-year property portfolio building plan and am looking forward to enjoying even more of the lifestyle that that recurring income will provide for me.

Loran Northey www.paramountcoaching.com

I saw Vicki talk last night at a property networking event, bought her book and woke up early today to read it. I was so excited – I have properties already but the money from banks has run out and I am starting a new business, so need to put all my cash into that at the moment.

So I have been struggling with how to get back into the property market with absolutely no money. People I talk to don't believe it can be done, but Vicki is a very ethical person and she knows her stuff. If you have been using the old 'I don't have enough money to get into property' excuse, then you now have nowhere to hide as Vicki explains how EVERYONE can get into property. One of the best property books I have read!

Fiona Howarth

Just finished your 'manual' on how to raise money and I have put it straight to work and raised £50k from a neighbour who recently sold an inherited house. The book also gave me the idea/confidence to ask the divorced owner of a property I am currently buying what he intends on doing with the money! (He had already bought another property.) He came to the conclusion that it would be better to invest his £100k with me. You are right when you say it is a huge responsibility. Thanks for being there.

Francis Dolley

I would recommend this book to anybody wanting to invest in property or expand their existing portfolio. Vicki has done a fantastic job of gathering and sharing the essential tools needed for anybody serious about creating a stable and successful property business. What is also valuable about this book is the fact that she has brought insights and lessons from some of the UK's leading property investors, coaches and trainers - outstanding.

Dr Rohan Weerasinghe, entrepreneur, investor and author www.rohanlive.com

Vicki, I ordered your book last week and it arrived yesterday. I started to read it at 10.30pm last night so wanted to message you to say a great big thank you as I couldn't put the book down. I found it to be written in a clear, honest and easy to understand manner, so here's a great big THANK YOU. On a negative note I am blaming you for my baggy and puffy eyes this morning. I blame you for this because if the book had not have been so good, I would have turned the lights out at 11pm.

Margret Agius

I can't recommend it enough. I have now read it twice and still feel a third time is required – YES there is that much information! Each time I refer to the book, I take out of it a new gold nugget of information.

Paulo De Silva

Many, many thanks for your book. It has been an inspiration and pushed me towards further action. I have found that it not only reinforced previous learning but made clear areas which I was unsure of before.

Gerry Harrington

Vicki comes into property writing from a radically different approach. Some people write a property book full of repetition, some are writing about an American market or a property market of a year or two ago, which is no longer there, and others tell you all the technical stuff but with little humanity. If you are new to the idea of property investing, then this is the place to start as Vicki takes a rounded approach, assuming that you are human, vulnerable and not necessarily minted. In the past boom years, even complete beginners could buy anything anywhere and the rise in the market flattered their abilities. Like us, Vicki came in to property relatively recently, so we have bumped in to her at numerous seminars and events.

Vicki is a brilliant networker and gives such care and attention to everybody she speaks to that she simply has earned the respect of everybody she associates with. It is refreshing to learn from an author who is still very much hands on and one of us, rather than lighting the way from the top of the tower from dim and distant memory. Don't be tempted to gloss over the personal development aspects of the book, which Vicki was brave enough to put at the beginning, because while the reader may want to be shown where the money is, in reality you need to talk to a property investor who will share their knowledge and experience and may just be that missing link you are looking for.

Steve Green

Contents

Foreword   xi

Acknowledgements   xiii

Introduction: Training and education versus understanding; information versus knowledge   1

Section 1	The power of the mind – success or failure, the choice is yours	11
	Chapter 1 Active responsibility – a new way of living	13
	Chapter 2 It's time to think about thinking	27
	Chapter 3 From thinking to doing	37
Section 2	Understanding the economic environment	59
	Chapter 4 The business of investing	61
	Chapter 5 Money – the reality	79
	Chapter 6 The rules – facts and figures	95
Section 3	Becoming a property business owner	103
	Chapter 7 Getting practical	105
	Chapter 8 Running the numbers – what makes a good deal?	123
	Chapter 9 Understanding the service you are offering	137
	Chapter 10 The contract and the paperwork	149
	Chapter 11 So, to summarise the whole book…	163
	Glossary	169
	Bibliography	171
	Moving forward	173

This book is dedicated to my dear friend Sally, whose life ended before we could see all our dreams come to life.

I miss you.

Foreword

One of the great benefits of being a transformational coach, entrepreneur and international speaker is that I get to see people rise like the phoenix, often from challenging circumstances, and make beautiful and positive changes to their own lives. Vicki Wusche is a shining example of this. What I love most about what Vicki has chosen to do, is that she has taken her journey and experiences and shared them with others in a clear and engaging way. It is my belief, that at this moment in time, the world needs more inspirational teachers; which is why her message is so important.

I first met Vicki in 2007 at a Wealth Education conference; and then later, through her journey of wealth and personal development education, we met at several other events. At each event, I was presenting and sharing my personal experience and knowledge; Vicki took the time to approach me and ask questions and was hungry to grow. She was never afraid to ask and always passionate to learn. It is my belief that this is one of the essential characteristics of anyone evolving beyond just a physical existence – the desire to expand from within. If you are open to learning, then this book will enable you to do exactly that.

In my first book, *Turning Point*, I wrote 'the first step to change is *awareness*'. Through the pages of this book, Vicki has truly helped the reader to raise their awareness of the important elements of not just buying investment property, but developing a business around long-term wealth. This is an essential stage in the evolution of anyone creating long-term business and financial security. If your path is one that involves YOU taking control of your financial future, and not relying on external circumstances to create your freedom, then you will derive great benefit from reading and applying the principles shared within this book.

Make More Money from Property shows a great balance between Vicki's own personal experiences and practical, hands-on tools that you can apply to your personal finances, your existing property business model and to the structure of your business for your life in the future. As you journey through this book, you will discover a shift from a mindset of wanting to make a positive impact on your financial circumstances, through to how to manifest that dream into the real world. The last section of the book provides practical approaches that work – if you are prepared to work at them. It is simple to read and presented in a clean, easy-to-process format. Vicki has gathered together knowledge from her own teachers together with her own personal experiences and insights – a great formula. I would recommend that you read it once, then read it again with a focus on where you are now and what you need to apply immediately.

I would like to share one personal message: Success is not a race; as you read these teachings, allow yourself to digest and apply them. There will be challenges and times when you may not quite 'get it'. Push on – allow your inner mind to search for the answers and they will reveal themselves. Trust that you have everything within you to grow and learn and to live your true greatness. That is the path that Vicki has taken and I know it is her belief, as it is mine, that you can enjoy the same journey of growth. *Enjoy* the teachings of the following pages and the process of making more money from property.

Yours inspirationally,

Dr Rohan Weerasinghe

www.rohanlive.com

Acknowledgements

One day I will write a book of gratitude and just list all the wonderful people I have been so blessed to meet and to have been supported by.

I will mention just a few here, there are many more and if your name is not listed please know that I am still eternally grateful.

First to Sue Richardson, my publisher, without whose help none of this would be possible. Her insights into the business, strategy, marketing and world of books have helped me raise the standard of this book to new heights.

Clare Gillbanks – her marketing and organisational skills are beyond compare. The lines between client, friend and colleague are blurred.

Loran Northey, my friend, business partner, supporter and critic, coach and conscience. I am so grateful, Loran – I appreciate everything you do to help me be the best I can and drive us to greater business success.

Hannah Liversidge, my tireless VA/PA that has helped me burst into the 21st century with ease. You are both my right and my left hand – thank you.

Then to just a few of the many others that have helped me:

- To everyone who bought my first book *Using Other People's Money: How to Invest in Property*. If you have not bought it, here is a cheeky link: http://bit.ly/OPM-Book1

- To every testimonial received for this book and the last.

- To every teacher, trainer, speaker I have ever heard.

- To every author I have ever read.

- To the many hosts of property events that have invited me to speak, especially John Cox, Sylvia and Juswant, Sue Elkington and Maksoom Bakhash and Robin Shaw and Simon Cartright, friends, supporters and amazing people.

- To all the fabulous people that I have met through networking at property events and through Ecademy especially; William Buist, Judith Germain, Georgina Lester, Penny and Thomas Power, Daniel Priestley, Darren Shirlaw, and so many others.

- To my technical supporters and advisors Andy Phillips and John Regis.

- And to John Cassidy for the most amazing photos – thank you.

I must make a special mention to Rohan Weerasinghe for his support and amazing foreword – Rohan is a perfect example of a good man; successful, supportive, caring, genuine and a great family man – I am lucky to have met him.

And finally to keep this brief; thanks to my parents, sister, beautiful and brilliant daughters Kimberley and Charlie and, last but not least, my darling and much loved Bob. My tireless supporter, the man with the most patience in the world – 'everyone needs a Bob' – I love you so much.

I love you all so much, thank you!

Introduction

Training and education versus understanding;
information versus knowledge

Introduction

Training and education versus understanding; information versus knowledge

£1,000s and £1,000s – are you getting a return?

If property training companies are training thousands of people on how to invest in property – the theory and techniques of how to invest in property – then why are so few people actually taking action and buying property? Also, why are so few people seeing a return on the thousands of pounds that they are spending to get this information?

It is because there is a difference between information and knowledge; a difference between training and understanding. 'If the brightest minds… got the best financial education money can buy, why are we in a massive financial crisis?' (Robert Kiyosaki, *An Unfair Advantage: The Power of Financial Education*, 2011, p27).

Information, like training and education, is what you receive when you go to school. Teachers teach you – in theory – out of context. Please do not misunderstand me; I am not disregarding all property training courses. There are some good courses and there are numerous people who will achieve success, regardless of the teacher or teaching techniques. Knowledge and understanding comes from experience – current real world experience – contextualised, because you are living in the moment.

In his book, Kiyosaki writes about his experience as a fighter pilot in the Vietnam War. He explains that he was well trained by his flight school trainers but he did not know how to repair his plane, nor did he understand the 'geo-political-economic' issues that were driving the war. Kiyosaki simply understood that 'All I was trained to do was fly; shoot and follow orders. Press the right button, and people died. Press the wrong button, and I died.' (p28).

The same is true of so many people once they leave a property training course. They have learnt a variety of strategies in a theoretical context. They do not know and understand the 'geo-political-economic' landscape that today's successful and professional property investors are fighting in. Buy the right property and they will have cashflow; buy the wrong property and they will die financially. This is because they have been trained, they have information, but they don't yet have the knowledge and understanding that comes with experience.

What is happening in our world? This is a coming of a new order, a new age. Not just a transition from the agricultural age to the industrial age to the information age. This is different. This is about different ways of thinking on a global scale in a world that is so interconnected that what happens in Japan, Africa or America is as relevant to your personal household as if your neighbours played loud music through the walls or parked across your drive.

Being trained by people who are not currently buying in today's real world economy is a recipe for disaster. I would go further and state that listening only to people who started their portfolios in a time of boom, plentiful lending and remortgaging strategies that led to many people having zero equity in a portfolio is also a poor recipe.

The economy is 'doomed'

The world economy, our country and possibly even some individuals are 'doomed'. Why? Because everything is interconnected:

- An American homeowner defaults on their mortgage, the bank collapses... the country faces bankruptcy as others default on an incomprehensible scale... the government cuts the budget and you lose your job; or...

- A lender rescinds your business overdraft without warning and you can no longer buy resources or pay staff to fulfil your order book; or...

- Interest rates rise and the cashflow from your portfolio dries up, leaving you unable to pay the mortgage... the portfolio is repossessed along with your family home...

Is this the future you want?

Do you just have information and strategies or do you have the knowledge and understanding to make the right decisions in a dynamic, exciting and volatile economic environment? Are you learning from people who started to build their wealth in these uncertain times – were they like you with little or no savings?

This is such an exciting time. Millionaires are created in times like this. Those who know how to use other people's money to leverage, and take action on that knowledge, will create significant investment portfolios that will provide for them and their families for generations to come. (See Vicki Wusche, *Using Other People's Money: How to Invest in Property*, 2010.)

Those prepared to let go of outdated information and beliefs and let a new body of knowledge and understanding take its place will be able to lie back and enjoy life.

Are you prepared to think differently about how you can create wealth, financial security and financial stability?

The aim of this book is to help you leverage your knowledge, and to leverage my knowledge and understanding. It is to help you develop your financial and business education and become a successful professional property investor and business owner.

The future is not about 'me first and stuff you'; it's going to be about 'we can do it – I am doing it – come on, join me and take action'. Take active responsibility for *your* life, *your* future, *your* wealth and income.

Do you want to make money from your property knowledge?

I was taught three crucial lessons about property:

1.   Buy at discount;
2.   Circulate your money; and
3.   Cashflow, cashflow, cashflow!

While I do believe wholeheartedly in these three fundamental rules, I also believe that I was misled.

In my experience, the detail lying behind these headline rules is costing you money and lots of it!

- Have you spent money on property training (maybe, like me, as much as £10,000–£20,000)?
- Have you still not seen a return on that investment?
- How many potential deals are you wasting because they don't fit the criteria you were taught?

For me, this really came to a head when someone contacted me through Facebook and asked me to send them the details of all of my deals over the last 6–12 months for analysis. They said that they had not been able to find any deals where they could get all of their money back within six months. I am not surprised! House prices and lending rules are just a few of the hurdles to be negotiated.

In the last two years, I have only been able to get all of my money back out of a deal within months on four out of over 30 properties bought for myself and bespoke clients. I achieved it on those four specifically because I negotiated a commercial funding deal with my bank to enable me to replicate the old 'Mortgage Express' style of buying for cash and then remortgaging – although over an extended timescale of 7–10 days. More importantly, what deals were being missed in pursuit of the goose that laid the golden egg?

The aim of this book is to share what I have learnt about property investing over the last three years so that you can:

- Learn the truth about investing in this new and constantly evolving economic market;
- Leverage your knowledge, skills, experience and passion to develop a phenomenal cashflowing property investing business; and
- Be living the life of your dreams within 18 months.

Unlike many people in the market today, I don't have a massive property portfolio that I can remortgage and release capital to buy property. When starting out, I was not prepared to commit mortgage fraud and lie to lenders so that I could own a property with no equity and poor cashflow. I started with a pot of £80,000 contributed by family members. I turned this into our first five properties that generated an average net cashflow of £1,000 per month. This was a massive 15% return on investment (ROI) – you definitely can't achieve this today via the banks or stock market. Even allowing 25% for disasters, voids and repairs, the investment would still return 11.25%.

What I have discovered is that building a successful property business requires three things:

1. A business mindset;
2. An understanding of the economic environment; and
3. Knowledge on how to turn the theory into an active and personal cashflowing strategy.

Are you ready to step up your game?

This book is designed to give you a head start at creating your own cashflowing property business. In my business, I focus on property sourcing as a business model. This enables me to focus on buying fantastic cashflowing investment properties for myself and, when my cash is busy, I turn to buying for my bespoke clients. They, in turn, pay me for my knowledge, experience and skill, which provides me with more cash to invest back into property.

Throughout the chapters of this book, I will often make reference to the fact that these are new and unpredictable times, both economically and politically. It is vital that you consider this in all that you read, both in this book and others. In addition, it is vital that you consider this in every decision that you make both now and in the future. Why? Because how someone built their portfolio in 2005, 2006 or even 2007 bears no relation to how you can start or grow your portfolio now. The 'no money down' (NMD) strategies of 2008–2009 are dead. Yes, we should aim to invest and circulate our money, of course, but not to the detriment of cashflow, equity, good deals and common sense.

We have moved from a period of 'mad investing' (where over-valued properties were over leveraged with 100% funding and now fail to provide significant cashflow) to a period of 'bad investing' where, as the availability of funds started to shrink, some investors became 'creative' and learnt to deceive and circumvent the lending requirements and rules – again leading to over-leveraged properties that risk negative equity and even zero cashflow in the near future.

I started my property investing business in June 2008, though I will admit I did not recognise it as a business then. I completed on my first independently sourced property in August 2008. Over the following four months, I faced more challenges than I could ever have thought imaginable and learnt more than I thought possible. I will cover many of those insights as we progress through the book.

It is crucial to note that when times (and lending) get tough, we need to be more determined to be successful. I, too, became creative in my financing strategies during 2009. However, instead of wandering into the grey areas of mortgage fraud and deception to trick the lenders, I looked for other ways to continue investing. I learnt how to use other people's money to invest in property (see my first book, *Using Other People's Money*).

This book moves on from the specific strategies that I explored and used during that time to explain the business critical skills that are transferable to any business model you choose. The skills that I gained have enabled me to grow my sourcing business into a bespoke high-value service. I have also developed a property training business to share my knowledge and experience more widely, and help investors like you to reach financial freedom as easily and pain-free as possible. I remember saying when I spoke to the Berkshire Property Meet in January 2010, very specifically, that 'I didn't want to create a business...'. I was wrong and misguided. Building a business is crucial to succeeding (even surviving) the next 5–7 years.

So, whether you are new to investing or experienced, this book is packed full of ideas and practical steps to help you turn your property knowledge into a business that can give you the 'lifestyle, cashflowing dream-machine' you wish for – all you have to do is work hard.

'Fortunately, there are many ways to financial heaven. I have found my way... It is up to you to find your way. This book is merely a guide, not an answer book, because in the real world there are no right answers... Only answers that work for you.'

Robert Kiyosaki – *An Unfair Advantage: The Power of Financial Education*, 2011, p20

'Being a leader means doing things on your terms. Being a loser means not getting people to follow you.'

Tony Robbins – NAC, June 2011

'Any business has to make money... they get lost in turnover, spreadsheets, and the future... they need money this week!'

Lord Alan Sugar – NAC, June 2011

'The cause of any [business] failure is a defocusing from the most important thing – are we making any money?'

Lord Alan Sugar – NAC, June 2011

'Why hope when you can learn, understand, take action, achieve results and get stronger? I am not a helper. I am a teacher, a tough teacher that some won't be able to handle. I don't mince words, I rock most boats, I profess action, and I demand hard work today for freedom and happiness tomorrow.

...I know some people won't step up. They are simply too lazy, too scared, too comfortable or are basking in the lull of false security to take charge of their lives. Some will come around. And when they do, I'll be there... I have many doors and every one of them is open to the willing, no matter their standing in life. Taking control all starts with a dream.'

Rich Dad – mission statement read at the start of each
game of CASHFLOW, Robert Kiyosaki

Section 1

The power of the mind – success or failure,
the choice is yours

Chapter 1

Active responsibility – a new way of living

This chapter explains how you can take charge and create your future. It acts as an introduction to this radical new way of thinking about property investment. I will walk you through changes in understanding that you will immediately recognise as sensible and obvious, so obvious that you will adopt them with ease. Not in a dreamy unrealistic, intangible way, but by taking *active responsibility* for your financial future.

I will explain what responsibility will mean in your life – and how it will empower you to create your future. I will show you how leverage is the most powerful tool we can use as professional property investors, and once this concept is understood you will never see money in the same way again. I will state the patently obvious – that action is what gets results. So why do so many people not have enough passive income or recurring income to give them financial security?

Active responsibility – a new way of living

If I asked you to tell me the story of your life to date, what would you say? Would you start with the negative or positive things about your life? We all love a story – rags to riches, failure to success (though reading the newspapers sometimes I think people prefer stories describing failure rather than success).

What I believe and how I behave today is as much my story as the 'historical' fact that I used to be a university lecturer, was made redundant and had been homeless. The thoughts and beliefs I have now have shaped business – they are positively influencing my financial futur

Taking active responsibility for your financial future require understanding and implementation of responsibility, levera income, action, contribution and self-preservation. I will ask you to question the way you think, even to revise what you believe, and change what you do or don't do.

This is such an important concept – it is more like my life philosophy. I have continually improved and developed it for my own purpose since I first became aware of it in 2007. I discovered the foundations of this approach to life when I went to a personal development seminar one weekend in late 2006. I started to understand how my mind worked and why I was the way I was. I learnt about critical concepts from the world of economics, psychology and neural sciences. Over the intervening years, I have brought together the thoughts and ideas of lots of philosophers, psychologists and thinkers into a personal 'soup' or recipe for success.

The first earth shattering concept I came across was responsibility.

The underlying science is that our minds are bombarded with millions of bits of information on a nanosecond-by-nanosecond basis. We would literally go insane if we had to deal with it all on a conscious level. So, very cleverly, we have been designed to have a conscious and a subconscious brain.

As information is presented, we subconsciously *filter* it into what our mind thinks we need to know consciously and what we don't. Our breathing, the texture of the chair we're sitting on, the touch of our clothes are all dealt with on a subconscious level, unless something out of the ordinary happens. I came to understand that some of these filters are about self-preservation – like breathing and our hearts pumping.

Some filters are created to preserve us because of past experiences. For example, we don't – or not many or us – put our hands on a hot pan. This may be because our mother shouted a warning or because we burnt ourselves in the past, causing pain. The mind then protects us from doing that same or similar action again.

So everything you do (or don't do) is either consciously or subconsciously ...led by you. Therefore, if you feel resistance, fear or apprehension about a certain action, it might be because somewhere in your past you had a negative feeling or warning about it, or simply lack information about it today. You might even feel resistance to this concept... are you now wondering why?

This means that everything you have or do in your life today is as a result of decisions you have or have not taken in the past. Therefore, if you are happy with your life, then it is because of you – *you* did that. If you are dissatisfied with your life, then that is also because of you – *you* did that too.

When I grasped this concept, I recognised that if everything in my life is of my doing (based on the knowledge and understanding I had at the time), then everything I want is also possible – I just have to consciously decide that I want it. This is such an empowering thought – it means I have complete control over the outcome of my life. I can design, build, have and live my life any way I want to.

You too can design, build, have and live your life – you just have to decide on the type of life you want. At this point, you can go down one of two paths: you can create a future life based on what you don't have in your life right now – seeing only the gaps; or you can choose to create a life that is grateful for everything you have and focuses on creating even more wealth, health and happiness. Which is more empowering?

The first step is to design the life you want and, sadly, 'filters' can get in the way here. Some people have negative thoughts, emotions and feelings about money, success or wealth. You weren't born like this – it was learnt from parents and peers of a past generation – people who were doing the best they could with the knowledge and resources that they had.

Some people have issues around failure and success. Sadly, much of this is taught to us in school. The aim of this book is not to teach you neurolinguistic programming (NLP), as there are excellent books, courses and coaches that can do this. I do, however, recommend that you take action to address any of those 'little voices' that plague you and hold you back, otherwise they will become like balls of lead around your ankles and drag dramatically on your goals and success.

For now, I want to move forward from the concept that you can control the outcome of your life. I have decided the life I want to live – I can amend, update and even enhance this regularly throughout my life as I have new ideas and see new opportunities. This is something that you will be able to do by the end of Section 1 (if not before). I suggest that, as you feel ready, you put the book down and take out some blank paper and write whatever comes into your head – notes about what you would like to be, have or do in your life or what you imagine in your dreams. You can choose. You can enhance, improve and even rewrite your future again and again if you want as your world opens to the possibilities that you can create.

Compounding – the art of leverage

The second concept that struck me was economics. I'm not referring to the type of economics I tried to study at school, not the supply and demand of business, although that is ever present in all of our lives whether or not we know it. I refer to economics in the form of leverage. Understanding the principle that if I have a specific number of resources (and let's use bank notes as an example), then once donated or spent they are gone from my hands. However, if I leverage (increase) those resources in some way, then I can have more bank notes in my hands which I can then donate or spend and still have my original amount left.

The following table shows the principle of doubling £1 every day for 21 days until very quickly it is over £1,000,000. Note how for the first 11 days nothing much is happening; there is no real impact of the doubling process. Then, all of a sudden, between days 17 and 21 the money starts to multiply on a massive scale.

Day	Amount (£)
1	1
2	2
3	4
4	8
5	16
6	32

7	64
8	128
9	256
10	512
11	1,024
12	2,048
13	4,096
14	8,192
15	16,384
16	32,768
17	65,536
18	131,072
19	262,144
20	524,288
21	1,048,576

My spending habits prior to understanding this principle were the same as any middle-class, reasonably well-off person, even though I was a single mum with a part-time job. If we wanted or needed something and we could afford it, we bought it. I loved to buy clothes, shoes and necklaces in particular, but I hated shopping and trying on clothes. Therefore, I would literally buy a couple of thousand pounds worth of clothes at a time on my credit card and then try them on at home in comfort with a glass of wine. I would do this two or three times a year. Did I need that many clothes or shoes? Did I wear that many clothes? Are there still boxes of brand new shoes in my cupboard? Let's move swiftly on from that question!

What about the money – where is it? Gone, of course, and with it the opportunity to become wealthy and financially free. I had no money left to invest. I had no idea that I could or should invest. In the action of spending money on consumer items, the opportunity to leverage and create even more wealth was also spent.

In light of this knowledge, I now clearly understand that every latte, every pair of shoes, even the odd necklace has to be bought with money that has already been leveraged, with my recurring income, money I did not trade my hours for. Now when I make a purchase I am not touching my capital.

This knowledge led me to the next series of critical lessons that helped me to develop the concept of active responsibility – the power to radically take charge of your life.

Just before I discuss this topic, can I ask you to see taking charge of your life as a wonderfully positive thing? Simply put, it means you won't have to sit rocking in a urine-stained chair in some institution for the old and unwanted, or be a drain and burden on your family. You will have the power, money and freedom to choose how you live your life – right through to a very happy old age.

Recurring income – you have to work for it

I dislike the term 'passive income' because no regular income is truly passive – there still needs to be work that takes place prior to the system or asset working for you, and there still needs to be a level of monitoring and checking to keep the cash-generating machine working. This is why I prefer the phrase 'recurring income'. Recurring income is the rent that is paid into my bank account every month and I don't have to trade my time working, speaking or writing to acquire it. I do, of course, monitor and manage it though.

The important point here is to move away from trading your time for money – because that is always going to limit your growth. Even if you charge £10,000 per hour, you can still only work so many hours a day or a week. More importantly, once you have created the lifestyle that you want to live, having to trade lots of hours for money will mean that you have less time for the things you want to experience.

There are a number of ways that people can invest their resources, time, knowledge and money to create income that is not related to the trade of hours.

The stock market

This is not for me. I can't influence the value of a share and whether it's Forex or trading it still smacks of gambling to me. It lacks control and certainly does not enable me to use other people's money. No bank will give you a mortgage on a share, which might indicate that lenders do not consider them a good lending risk or an actual asset.

Internet marketing

I have definitely had a go at this over the years, but found it dull when taken out of context. It didn't require me to meet or speak to people, or indeed even to leave the house. I find those long, long sales letters boring – I don't read them and I don't understand how the research can say they work. If I could not get with the programme, then it was never going to work for me.

I will come back to this later as a brilliant form of marketing with a focus on creating websites to sell products and passion and a team of outsourcers to do the technical boring bit.

Business

Okay, business sounds do-able, although I need to be careful not to create another job for myself – this time one of managing staff. So I looked at multi-level marketing (MLM). I could see the definite benefits of leveraging other people's time as a resource. The issue for me came from the initial time it takes to build the team to that critical mass that means you don't have to work. I estimated that I would need to invest 2–3 years (depending on my initial contact database size) of my time to build and support my team to success.

During that time, I would have to work long hours for a very low rate of return. I worked out that I was earning £2.50 per hour – not a motivator for me. It is an excellent business if you already have a full-time job or you are a student looking to create a recurring income stream to buy your initial freedom. It works brilliantly if you coach people around their health and then sell products through MLM to your target group, for example. I am always happy to refer people on to my original team members. I am not convinced though that it works for the average person looking to create an income, unless, as I mentioned, you already have a large contact database or the product is synergistic with your current business.

I actually started to invest in property straight away once I recognised that leverage was the key to financial freedom. I could see that I could borrow other people's money. In fact, I *had* to as I didn't have any savings. I could leverage any money borrowed to both pay off the cost of borrowing and still leave me with a profit. The initial capital debt would be cleared either by the sale of the asset or the later (much later) rise in asset value.

Eureka! I could design my own destiny, create my dream world and do it all without having to trade my hours. Better still, I could use other people's money and make a profit – an on-going 'recurring' income. Now all I had to do was 'do it'. Of course, this 'business' would take time to set up, but the cashflow, ROI and return on my time was almost immediate – certainly a lot quicker than with the MLM businesses.

Action – the only way to be successful

Now comes the final ingredient that takes responsibility, leverage and recurring income as concepts and turns them into a recipe for financial freedom. The ingredient is action. You can't take consistent and progressive action unless you understand how your mind works and accept the concept of responsibility. *You* are responsible for the outcomes in your life – good or bad. If you don't like the outcome, change the decision and make a better one next time. Learn from your mistakes – they are just a lesson, not something to fear.

Who would you look upon more favourably? The person who sat safely taking no risks and living a mediocre life or the person who took action, learnt, explored, got knocked down, but got up again and gave life their all – living life to their full potential and beyond?

If you take action and responsibility but you don't understand about leverage, you will spend your capital and run out of money – yours and other people's money – very quickly. If you don't understand about passive or recurring income, you will just create another job for yourself and find that you have no time to enjoy the future you dreamed of and may even have created. Time with our loved ones is precious and all too short – having fun and learning new things is the greatest gift we as humans can have. Loved ones, fun and new things will be different for all of us, but none of it will be possible if you don't take active responsibility for your life and the lives of those who depend on you.

Who are you really helping?

At this point, there are two smaller inter-linked, but still important, lessons: contribution and self-preservation. They go back to the concept of values – what is important to us in any given context. Many of us have a strong desire to help others. For some, it manifests as charity work or contribution; for others, it is 'telling' them how they can do what we have done.

I strongly believe that we have a moral duty to help others and that it is a natural instinct to help. There is a belief that the more you give, the more you get – so, if you give time, you get more time; if you give money, you attract more money; if you share your time, money, love and knowledge, you are rewarded with a truly wealthy life.

I remember being dreadfully unhappy in the final months before my marriage ended – unhappy because this was neither the life I wanted nor how I ever imagined I would be treated by another person. Even more upsetting, what sort of a role model was I for my two daughters? Did I want them to grow up and see this downtrodden miserable woman – probably unkempt as all self-confidence left her – unemployed and possibly depressed? Is that what I wanted for my two baby girls?

What had gone wrong? My mother always worked hard, supported my father and loved him. They never argued in front of me or my sister; we were a united and loving family. My mother had owned her own business before she had children and now worked for an employer, but was clearly enhancing the business with her work ethic and ideas. My father was a master tailor and ran his own business. (I use the past tense here but I am blessed that they are both still alive and well.)

I remember writing 'letters' to my then husband to explain why I was unhappy – I was able to articulate it clearly in writing. It would have caused another violent argument to explain using the spoken word. I never sent the letters – it was as though I was having a conversation with another part of me that needed to make a decision, but was afraid. I needed to leave the situation, but I didn't have the knowledge and understanding that I have now. I was afraid of unseen consequences – I was responsible for two other lives and needed to make the right choice. I allowed the fear, overwhelming pressure and stress to paralyse me.

I realised that I needed to leave and started to make mental plans – working each plan out and then evaluating the consequences. Actually, I was afraid on so many levels: afraid to stay and afraid to go. In the end, the decision was taken from me and I literally nearly paid for my indecision with my life. It had taken over 18 months before circumstances – violent circumstances – stepped in and gave me a push!

When I did leave so many people helped me: friends and their friends and families. Donations of kitchen equipment or second-hand clothes for the girls were received as treasured gifts. I became so incredibly grateful that I wanted to repay the kindnesses – I had been given the gift of a new life.

I helped everyone (whether or not they wanted it). Everyone from the person in the queue next to me to fellow students and total strangers. I helped everyone else so much that I forgot about my daughters, whose precious lives I had set about rescuing in the first place. I forgot about my parents who supported me through incredibly difficult times. I even forgot about my father who suffered physically at the hands of my ex-husband! What about my sister and the impact on her life? How did I forget them? I was so busy giving my time and attention to everyone else rather than focusing on those people nearest to me who loved me. Well, that's not totally true as I do remember becoming obsessed with doing my mother's ironing and cleaning while we lived with her – it was a way of saying 'thank you' and paying back the kindness.

I spent close to the next 10 years helping 'others' (mostly the students and businesses I worked with at the university) achieve their goals, dreams and desires and did nothing to directly support my family towards greater financial security and happiness. Why? Because my values were all about giving back and supporting others to have the opportunity I was given – the opportunity of a new and wonderful life.

I first heard the story of the aeroplane oxygen masks at a seminar in 2007. On an aeroplane, the hostess explains that in the event of an accident the oxygen masks will fall from the compartment overhead. She tells you to put on your own mask first. If we did not hear that instruction, the natural instinct for many of us would be to check on others around us first. Does that resonate with you? What would you do?

In fact, if you stop to help others before ensuring your own air supply, you may well pass out and die. If you put on your own mask (financial or oxygen-giving) first, then you can help the 6–10 people around you and they can help the 6–10 around them. In fact, by putting on your mask own first you could save the whole plane!

The second interwoven complexity is that in our desire to help we can be prone to 'telling', to sharing the results of our lessons in the honest attempt to help others not make mistakes. We need to remember that everyone has their own values; everyone has their own unique pasts and their own unique futures. Not everyone will be at the same point in their journey of life as you, not even your own family, especially brothers and sisters.

People need to travel at their own speed. If you are moving more swiftly to financial security and financial freedom, leave the door open for others to follow. Let them see the path you have taken so they can follow when they are ready. We all have to learn our own lessons. How many times did you sit in school and hear the teacher and understand the lesson, but know that people around you hadn't – or vice versa?

So, while we may have grasped the concept of active responsibility and know what we have to do to put it into action, others around us will not be able to take that step. They may lack the courage to overcome their fears or they may not be prepared to examine the beliefs that underlie their core values and create their results. We don't need to boast, brag or show off – we just need to be congruent and get on with living the dream life that we have created for ourselves and our immediate families. Then, when others are ready, you (the teacher) will be there, prepared to share all of your knowledge so that others may learn from your mistakes and successes, helping them to create their own version of a wonderful life.

Changing the future for our children's children

Our schools are failing our children and future generations on so many levels – I could write a book on that subject alone. To summarise, at a basic level the system is failing to teach even reading, writing and maths skills – core skills for any sort of future. At another level, there is no financial education whatsoever to prepare our young people for the real world. Children are theoretically being trained to be employees without an understanding of the geo-political-economic environment they are entering. As employees, they could add so much to any business if they understood world economics. Why? Because, unlike many of us, they understand the emerging new uses of technology – the interconnectedness of everything – so much better.

Schools train our kids to be employees – if they stay the course and learn the basics. That's not so bad because not everyone is ready to be an entrepreneur and run their own business. Many want the security of a job and we need people to serve us in the shops and heal us when we're sick. It might be nice if people could choose. Maybe those who don't feel that school or employment is a path for them would benefit from knowing that they have other options. Maybe they would recognise that self-employment, entrepreneurship or investment is the answer they are searching for.

What is criminal is not explaining to young people how money works and how to leverage it. My daughter and her boyfriend have just bought their first home together. They understood the techniques of a professional investor because I viewed the first few properties with them and explained, in context, how to offer, how to know what to offer, what research to do, what to look for and what questions to ask.

More importantly, they know that they will never sell this house. When they are ready to trade up, they will release equity and then rent this property to professional tenants because they have bought in the right location. They understand that they can take their current savings and leverage them for their own purposes. They understand about assets and liabilities. They understand about good debt and bad debt. They understand how to use credit cards to build credit ratings and not to make others rich by paying massive interest rates. They have a plan to buy their first investment property within the next 12 months.

It is your *duty* to prepare your children for the world because school and the educational system will not. Explain the principles you have read in this chapter:

- You can do anything you set your mind to – you have the power to decide your future.

- Once £1 is spent, it is gone for good – leverage and spend from revenue or capital gains.

- You can have a job and still create other income on the side – you can have a MLM business or internet business – you could write a book, create a product or offer another service.

- The 'system' is crumbling, therefore you must take active responsibility for your financial future – government cannot sustain a free education, healthcare and welfare system, and pensions are linked to a fluctuating stock market that government has no control over.

- There is good debt and bad debt, assets and liabilities. Learn the difference.

- When you want to learn something new, seek out someone who is doing it now, is being successful and is relevant. Not someone who did something in a different financial or economic climate that is worlds apart from now.

Lastly, I heard a great talk hosted by Triumphant Events about the stages of wealth, where the speaker, Darren Shirlaw, said that in every family there is a cycle of wealth. A generation that labours hard to create real money that the next generation uses and invests to create a recurring income. Then comes the third generation that is born into a wealthy family with no relationship to the money it relies upon and spends it – effectively losing it all.

I believe we go through that cycle as a country and an economy, but the cycles are moving faster. It is our job to *educate* our children and our children's children about money – how it works, how it flows. We all need to learn to tap into the rivers of money flowing around in our economy and make it work for us. How exactly we do that will change – originally it changed within a generation, then it changed within a decade and now it changes almost annually!

Teach your family about real money and relative money (see page 69). Teach them how to leverage, not to save. Teach them how passive income works and that it is not passive, it is in fact recurring income – because it needs love and attention to keep working.

Chapter 2

It's time to think about thinking

In September 2010, I decided to get off the work treadmill for a couple of weeks and to clear my diary. It felt as if I was so involved in the business, so close to it that I could no longer see where I was going. I knew what I wanted to achieve, but I just wasn't sure if I was heading in the right direction.

By encouraging you to slow down and even take a break from business for a couple of weeks, this chapter will show you how to tap into untold energy, focus and direction. I will explain the mechanical process, unravel some of the science and explain the results.

This chapter will explain how:

- Aligning your values with your business goals will virtually guarantee success, without anything else coming into play;

- Listening for and looking for messages from your subconscious is a path to opportunity and success;

- To filter for success and retrain your 'little voice' to be more supportive; and

- Writing your goals is a great tool to train your mind to focus on what you want to achieve.

Ultimately, you can choose whether or not you change your thinking but, as Henry Ford's wise saying goes, 'If you always do what you've always done, then you'll always get what you've always got'. If you are happy with your results so far, then great! However, I imagine that you are reading this book because you want to achieve even more success, wealth and happiness and that is going to require a change in thinking.

Life is getting faster, time is getting shorter. We rush to achieve and succeed. When do we make time to think and plan? This chapter is about thinking rather than planning – the stage that needs to come before planning. If you miss out the thinking stage of the planning process, then how will you know if you have considered the potential consequences of what you might be planning?

The mechanical process

I knew I wanted to write a second book and roughly knew what I wanted it to be about. What I didn't understand was how the book would fit into my business and, if it did, what that meant. My primary business is sourcing property, so why did I want to write a book? I decided that I needed some time to think – a period of relaxation and quiet contemplation.

That already sounds a bit strange. Actually, it was days crossed out in my diary when I could think, read, listen and learn instead of just doing all the time. It could be called 'strategic development', a very corporate sounding process. It is actually the art of thinking about your business – some working *on* it time rather than working *in* it.

The mechanical process that took place was easy – I crossed out three weeks in my diary and pledged to not make any appointments or meetings during that time. This was going to be time where I could 'choose' to do what I wanted rather than fulfil business-based 'obligations'. That is actually the key to the success of the process: choice not obligation; space and time not meetings and appointments. You need to be committed and strict with yourself, otherwise the outside world will creep in and steal your thinking time.

When I had my first 'business retreat' ideas flowed into (or out of) my head at a phenomenal rate and quality – a really 'mysterious process' and an unusual feeling. I often have ideas, but these were clear, inspired, ground-breaking business and life-altering realisations.

It was almost eight months later when I read Tom Evans's book *Flavours of Thoughts*: *Recipes for fresh thinking*, that I started to understand what I had accidentally enabled. In his book, Tom explains a new way to think about thinking. It really helped me to understand what had happened in September 2010 and why the 'experiment' had had such a phenomenal impact on my business. So much so that it prompted this most recent planned and more focused period of thinking, which in turn led to me writing this book.

What I had achieved was the space and time for my poor subconscious mind to share bits of information and ideas that it had filed away as not dramatically important in the moment they were experienced or thought. I allowed ideas to flow into my head. (From where they came: the super conscious, other minds, other lives, or just the energy that surrounds – I did not know.) As the pace of life slowed and the diary quietened, I could think more easily. I could hear my thoughts in the silence and they were good ideas! My thoughts helped me to see strategies and opportunities to grow my business. Once I had a clearer picture of my purpose, I was able to meet with Sue Richardson, my book publisher, and move forward.

What's important to you? You can choose what you value

I first studied NLP in 2007 and, as mentioned in Chapter 1, I have identified what I believe to be the three critical business skills needed to drive your business to the next level.

If you have read around this subject or been to events embodying NLP practice, then you will understand the concepts of 'values, attitudes and beliefs' and how they impact on our daily lives and how our subconscious mind operates a 'life-saving' filtering process to keep us safe and sane. If this is all news to you, then please explore this – I found Christopher Howard's book, *Turning Passions Into Profits,* very insightful, along with Dr Rohan Weerasinghe's more recent book, *Turning Point.*

I learnt that we can either live our lives at the effect, direction and impact of others, or we can take active responsibility for the decisions we make and change those that produce outcomes we do not desire.

Ultimately, you are responsible for everything that happens in your life, not your boss, parent, the government or the other driver – *you are responsible*. This is such an empowering realisation. You can choose to do anything you want, be anything you want, have anything you want – and change it if you don't like it!

Values are the traits and qualities that are important to you. When I first did this exercise, I realised that my values were all about helping other people, sharing and supporting. These are great qualities, yet they did not seem to help *my* family. This is why the air hostess story in Chapter 1 on page 23 is such an important metaphor. '...put on your own mask first' – the choice is save yourself and then the 6–10 people around you or pass out trying to help the person closest to you.

I realised that success, wealth and finances were not something that I had listed as important to me. With the support of my coach, I was able to change my thoughts and the things I valued. I will mention coaching later but, at this point, I want to emphasise how a good coach can dramatically impact on your success. I have worked with my personal coach, Johnnie Cass, since 2007, when I first studied NLP. As I gradually let go of limiting beliefs that held me back, my coaching sessions have changed emphasis and now hold me accountable for the goals I set.

Changing the way I thought and what I valued, in turn, changed my subconscious filtering mechanism – did I 'see' more opportunities or 'attract' them to me – I don't know. Within three weeks, I won a contract for £20,000 from a past contact. Within eight months, I had trained and bought my first investment property. Within 18 months, I was financially free! That is why understanding your values, getting them aligned and supporting your goals is crucial to your business and personal success. This is why getting the right coach can help support that process of change.

Aligning your values to your goals virtually guarantees success. A famous proverb says: 'A true warrior has all his horses face the same direction.' Your values are a critical part of your cavalry.

Messages – what is your subconscious trying to tell you?

I can't remember when I first read *The Celestine Prophecy* by James Redfield. It's a story about a man on a journey and how he learns to recognise signs and messages in the things that happen around him. Signs and messages from whom? Actually, it's more scientific than mystical. Remember, our senses are bombarded with information overload. To remain sane our subconscious mind filters this information so we don't have to consciously think to breathe or pump blood around our bodies. In the filtering process we may miss things, so our subconscious 'notices' signs, symbols, even words or music that might trigger a memory of something that passed us by unnoticed at a conscious level.

Our mind is such a wonderful and powerful tool, we just don't pay it enough attention. Sometimes 'messages' appear as a vague sense of awareness, other times we seem to 'see' the same thing over and over again. People repeat patterns in work or relationships and ask the question 'is this a message?' when they get the same results. Well, the answer is 'yes'.

Celebrity or success – what are you filtering for?

Lots of people read celebrity magazines, which have fuelled a whole media industry. So where in their filtering process did the message that 'success is desirable' become replaced with the message that 'celebrity is desirable'? What made people value celebrity? Maybe somewhere in their thinking patterns people have confused celebrity status (whatever that means) as an indicator of success and, to some maybe, it is the same thing.

Most of the general public read about the lives of people who marry and have babies, face lifts or public disputes. You, however, are most likely reading about how key business people created their businesses and overcame challenges to shape their thinking and achieve financial freedom. That is what sets you apart. Your filtering process is different. You value different things to the ordinary person on the street. You have created different rules about what is important to you (whether or not you are aware of this).

Now you can enhance that process and specifically filter for certain behaviours, traits or achievements by influencing your values, writing your goals and directing your education.

What are the voices telling you?

Limiting beliefs or the concept of 'the little voice' is both an NLP principle and a book by Blair Singer. The idea is that we all hear a voice (or voices) in our head. If you are asking 'what voice?', then that *is* the voice. Sometimes it can be negative or limiting. Ultimately, it is only doing its best to protect you.

The 'little voice' will kick in when the filtering process fails. If you either recognise an opportunity or fail to recognise something that might 'harm' you in some way, then the little voice will have to take charge and make clear any underlying fears or concerns.

Again, aligning your focus and values will help you to train your subconscious to know what is important to you. Writing your goals will make clear what you want to achieve. The process of thinking about and writing down your goals takes time, focus and thought. Your subconscious notices this as a significant activity and that ultimately impacts on what you value, filter and focus on. This can even help to quieten some of the more negative voices or limiting beliefs and sharpen your filtering process to recognise opportunities.

What did you dream about last night?

The little voice can also come to us in our dreams; here, it appears as images rather than words (although some people may have words in their dreams too). Dream analysis is a tool that enables you to analyse the remembered contents of a dream. It can be used as a specific tool to communicate with the subconscious part of our brains. I have an easy set of notes to follow (go to TheSourcersApprentice.com if you would like a copy) but, in brief, if you keep a note pad by your bed and then first thing in the morning make a note of what you remember, you might be able to start to see the messages that your subconscious wants to send you.

Now I am not sure what will come first: the chicken or the egg. In other words, I don't know if you will start to recognise opportunities and answers to challenges because you follow this process, or if by following this process you open a channel of communication with the subconscious mind. I don't think it matters as long as you gain a deeper understanding of something you previously didn't understand.

You don't have to understand everything I have just covered: from values and beliefs, limiting little voices, dream analysis or communicating with your subconscious through signs and dreams, goal writing and coaching – you might not even need to believe it all. Just be open to the idea that there are things that we don't completely understand. Having said this, these new ways of thinking (NLP and beyond) do have provable results. My life has changed dramatically since I decided to be open to these ideas – take them on board, test them out with an open mind and create my own recipe for success. Now you just need to take action on what you have learnt.

Bringing our thinking together

If you add all of this new understanding together, what you will have learnt is that there is a body of thought (or belief system) that believes there are three levels of consciousness:

- Our conscious mind, which may decide to have a cup of tea rather than coffee; it has the ability to make conscious choices.

- Our unconscious or subconscious mind, which controls our survival – from breathing through to flight or fight responses. This part of our brain also subconsciously influences our decisions. This may manifest itself as our inability to make a decision or take an action. It can also migrate into our conscious world as a 'little voice' that says: 'I wouldn't do that if I were you, it will only go wrong…'; 'you don't deserve to be successful – you never have been before…'; or it might appear as a garbled message in a remnant of a half-remembered dream.

- Our super conscious, which sits outside our body; it is the collection of all that is and all that was. (I admit I don't fully understand all there is to know on this topic. However, I remain open and inquisitive about the concept.)

The best bit is that I have worked out why I sometimes resist certain decisions or actions. By being in tune with my subconscious mind, listening, thinking and analysing, I have been able to regain control over my life in the last four years. This is something that you can achieve easily. One way is to accept that there were things you didn't know about before and you have simply become more vigilant and attentive for any messages.

If this topic area intrigues you as I know it will, then check out the resources at TheSourcersApprentice.com, the website that accompanies this book, and do some reading on the subject for yourself. Develop your own understanding – it may be different from mine because you may need to put emphasis on a different part of the thinking process.

What are the practical applications of all this thinking?

It boils down to three key points for me:

- By acknowledging that I have a little voice (in my case, a whole choir of voices) in my head and by listening out for them, I can start to tell when I am taking an action that at some level unsettles or scares me. By recognising this, I can think consciously about it and even double-check the decision. This is a very positive thing to do – self-affirming and appropriate. Once I am sure that I want to pursue that particular action, then I can acknowledge my little voice and thank it for helping me (that is an NLP technique that aims to reassure you at a subconscious level that you are working coherently towards a positive direction) and take appropriate action.

- When I face a challenge or become stuck for inspiration, I can use dream analysis. Then trust that I will understand what action I need to take next.

- I am alert to new learning and opportunities in my daily life. Again, these might be things that my subconscious mind has noticed or wants to share with me. That is why all my blogs contain stories with messages

– because I see them everywhere. My focus is clear. My aim is to develop even further my successful cashflowing property business and so my subconscious wants to help me in any way it can by pointing out things that will act as reminders, memory triggers and potential opportunities.

What new understanding could you tap into if you became more alert for signs that you had missed subconsciously in amongst the mass of information? What business opportunity, strategy or person could you connect with? What greater clarity and drive towards your goals could you achieve if your whole mind is working towards the same outcome?

I can remember my mother telling me that I think too much. A friend said the same thing to me just yesterday. My 'thought' is that, if you know what you want and believe, your thoughts can help you to achieve your goals. Can you ever think too much? Can you ever achieve too much?

We only understand and use less than 10% of our brain. Who is to say that any of what I have written is not true? If you can start to understand how you think and why you think the way you do…, if you can start to get your whole mind and body working together like a well-oiled machine, you could become an Olympic athlete in your own business.

After we have:

- Understood our thought processes;
- Recognised and mastered the little voice and so removed our limiting beliefs;
- Adopted empowering values and beliefs;
- Connected and worked in harmony with our whole minds;
- Analysed our dreams;
- Taken responsibility for our decisions and their outcomes;
- Learnt to leverage our resources;

The final component to all of this thinking is, of course…

- to take action.

The book by Jeff Olson, *The Slight Edge,* was amazing – it was written just for me. (Or it felt like it when I read it for the first time.) The author spoke of the compounding effect of making the 'right' decisions. It brought together the idea that I can influence and control my own future with the power of leverage. It reminded me that, from day to day, it is hard to see the progress that has been made, but as we look back from the future we can see the massive distances we have travelled.

I am a whole new person since the start of 2007. I'm not different – more rediscovered – I remember all my forgotten possibilities. All that I am now was always my potential. I had allowed others to steal my power, confidence, passion and determination. Starting at school with teachers saying I asked too many questions, to the bullying by other pupils, then to work colleagues and their spiteful gossip, through to unsupportive and disempowering employers, and finally to an ex-husband!

Now I know what I want to achieve. I know that I can achieve it on my own and even more quickly with the support and collaboration of the wonderful people I am surrounded by. Above all, my journey is my choice. I am powerful beyond measure and humbled by that knowledge.

I really want this chapter to enable you to see that you too are powerful beyond measure. Be humbled by that knowledge and then continue reading – pulling out vital pieces of knowledge or experience that will help you to speed along a less bumpy pathway to your financial freedom.

Chapter 3

From thinking to doing

Until now, I have hardly mentioned property investment other than as a casual frame of reference. This is because I spent a whole year before I was even ready to consider property investing gaining the basics of the knowledge and understanding I have just been discussing.

Well, that's not totally true because if I look back (isn't hindsight a wonderful thing?), I can see that property investment was a clear message or calling throughout my adult life, from working for a mortgage broker to looking at the differences between new build and older constructions and how people could leverage the value of certain properties over and above normal inflation rates. Even so, it still took many years of debate and discussion before I eventually took action, and then it was only to engage a sourcing agent to help me!

I certainly was not engaged at this point. I still was not doing anything about creating my own financial security because I simply did not have that as a concept I could even consider. I just gave a man our money and was lucky that he picked great investments for us.

That is why I work with my clients to develop their investment strategy so that they are engaged in the process. It is their responsibility because the wealth I help them to access will determine the shape of their future lives.

Once I understood this and then continued with my education around wealth, finances and the economy, I was ready to use property investment as my vehicle to financial freedom. Alongside gaining knowledge, both mental and technical, I was imagining my ideal lifestyle, my dream life. I knew how much money I needed to live that life and I knew what my days would be like – how I would spend my time. I created a picture and then added detail – I still add detail. That gave me my reason to invest in property. It gives me strength to overcome the inevitable challenges of doing something different to everyone else. It helps me to stay motivated and focused.

This chapter is going to take you on a journey. It will help you to map out your future, decide your financial needs, reach equilibrium and recognise how valuable your time is. By the end, you will have the outline of your personal financial strategy – the vital first step to creating your property business – to give you the strength to blast through the obstacles and challenges that may come to test your resolve.

The critical success factor in any business venture is your ability to keep going when others stop. That is of course providing you are on a path to success and have chosen the right strategies. I will cover the technical detail of property investing and running a successful property investment business in greater depth later on in this book in Section 3.

What does your cake look like?

I will use the analogy of a recipe (it must be lunchtime while I am writing). If you don't know what sort of cake you want to bake, then how do you know if you have the right ingredients? Come to think of it, are you even following a recipe that is relevant to you now? For example, if you want to eat more healthily or avoid wheat, is the recipe you are following going to give you the outcome you want?

Okay, so let's start from the beginning. What do you want your cake to look like – your life to look like? Are you interested in outdoor activities, travel, country living? Do you want to ease future financial pressures when your children go to university or you retire? Whatever you choose is fine; it is your life and your future. Just make sure it is *your* life and *your* future and not about buying a house for a relative. The reason I mention this takes us back to the concept of helping others. When I started investing, I did what many of you may be thinking about… I decided to buy my parents a new house in the country. When I actually spoke to my mother and asked her what she wanted, she said she didn't want to move!

This brings us to a section in the book where you need to be totally selfish for a few pages and put your needs above others. Focus on just *your* goals. Then you can add in contribution and wider family later.

So, if you have chosen *your* end goal (which may grow, develop and change before you even get there because you can make it even better if you want), what are a few of the steps you need to take along the way?

Now you have created an end goal you will need some interim goals to get you there – this is not so hard. My biggest dream is to dive in all of the warm water coral reefs of the world taking wonderful photographs and learning about the natural life of the sea. Photographs and marine biology were added to my dream as I started to develop my vision. This vision is actually a metaphor for a whole lifestyle needed to support it.

One of my business partners wants a donkey. A donkey to keep some horses company in a field at the back of his large house where he lives the life of his dreams with his family. The donkey is his metaphor – the anchor for his vision.

Now that I had my vision (my cake) I started to work out how much money I had coming in and how much I needed to live this lifestyle. I calculated very roughly what the shortfall was – this became my financial goal or, to stay with the metaphor, the 'shopping list of ingredients' I needed.

How much money do you really need?

Now I had a figure in mind. Initially, it was a rather easy and conservative number to achieve, but enough to buy me four scuba-diving holidays a year, along with a few UK-based long weekends for good measure. My initial personal target was £120,000 per annum. (I have since revised that number. As I achieve my previous target, I add a few more expensive holidays and increase my goal. I am not ready to retire just yet.)

It is all well and good to create targets of £1,000,000 per year, but I believe a realistic plan to achieve that would take a considerable time. Can you sustain your drive long enough to achieve it? I explain on pages 51–55 how I work out what I am worth in terms of the value of my time.

Before I do that, just look at the figure of £120,000 – that is £10,000 per month. That could be 40 properties giving £250 net profit per month on an assured shorthold tenancy (AST). It could be renovating and flipping a property every three months for £30,000 profit. It could be sourcing two properties a month for bespoke clients. Or it could be a combination of all of the above. All of this is achievable but still a stretch.

Each time I get close to my financial target and I feel my performance dropping, I revise the goal and stretch it further. If you set a goal for £1,000,000 per annum, you will need a staff team and a massive business to manage it. I want to scuba dive and spend time with Bob, my partner, and my family and friends – not sit at a computer or in an office managing a business. If you do, then that's fine. Think about the life you want to live as well as the money and make sure the two can work together in harmony.

Finding your financial equilibrium

Another process I went through was to make sure I understood my own current and immediate financial situation. Did our family income meet or exceed our expenses? Were our expenses as a family reasonable? Was every bill necessary? I realised that we were paying for an old decreasing term life insurance policy that still cost £65 per month, but would now only pay out a fraction of our mortgage. We also had four other life and health policies. So, after a careful review of our insurance needs, I cancelled a number of policies, including a family health care policy that included the girls but no longer provided them with cover. I saved £455 per month. That's just under two good buy-to-let property cashflows! I have already mentioned that I learnt about leverage and so changed my spending habits. This saved another £500 per month on average.

Next, I looked at our credit cards, credit reports and credit scores (see pages 46–48). By using a 0% strategy, I saved money and, in fact, made money. (See my e-book, *Managing Your Credit Cards, Scores and Reports* at

TheSourcersApprentice.com.) All of this research led me to a point where I understood our financial position. I also started to understand how money worked and flowed. I knew the life I wanted to live and how much money it would take to get there. I knew what I wanted my days to be like – how much time I was prepared to spend to maintain, sustain and enhance our wealth in the future. Now I could start to think about the technicalities of which strategy to pursue.

Understand why you want to invest in property. What image or dream is going to keep you going through the tough times? What is going to help you face the inevitable challenges that will come across your path to financial freedom? Knowledge, determination and focusing on success are what separate the successful investor from the ordinary person in the street.

Case study – from fearing redundancy to a life in the country

A mum of two was holding down two jobs to make ends meet. Her main employer was looking to make staff redundant and she hated her job. In fact, she recently told me that she realised it was 'killing' her. She already had some properties, but there was no equity and a negative cashflow, causing an even bigger leak in the family budget.

Her dream was to not have to work, to focus on her art and her children and, if possible, to move out of London. I helped her buy four cashflowing properties, restructure her finances and let out her residential home so that she could then buy another house out of London and change the quality of life for her family.

She knew what she didn't want and by working together we created her dream. I used my knowledge and understanding to act as a catalyst that ultimately changed her life. We still stay in touch and she regularly lets me know how amazing her life is, how happy she is and how much happier her children are. She took active responsibility for her life, understood leverage and took action – now she has the rest – the life of her dreams. We are already making plans to buy her a few more properties.

What you focus on is what you get

I have already explained that property investing was ringing so loudly in my ears that I had no choice other than to open the door to those possibilities. I have also explained why I do not pursue other business and investment models and part of that reason, or rather the major part, is focus.

There is a saying 'Focus on One Course Until Successful' (FOCUS). I spent many months explaining to my coach, Johnnie Cass, that I was focused. When he raised my lack of focus as a possible reason I was not getting the success I wanted, I argued back that I was like a juggler – I had three balls in the air, but at any one time I was only focused on the ball at the top of the cycle. Quite good I thought...

Months later, when I was miserable and still not achieving the success I wanted, I surrendered and it really did feel like that. I focused only on buying cashflowing property in one area in the north west of England – one strategy. I was scared – was I missing other opportunities? Everything I had tried before wasn't giving me the results I wanted, so I had to give this 'focus thing' a chance. Maybe Johnnie was right?

Everything changed. During 2009, on average I bought one or two houses per month. I also set up my first property-related business – a sourcing service for bespoke clients who had access to equity or savings but neither the time nor knowledge to invest in property themselves. I earned an additional £17,500 in sourcing fees and 'ready to invest' strategy development sessions. Focus was working for me – my surrender had paid off.

I speak to so many potential property investors and they all tell me how they are dabbling in other money-making opportunities. Some are doing MLM, a bit of internet marketing or they trade stocks. Chapter 1 explains about filtering out the overwhelming amounts of 'normal' information our brains have to cope with... yet some people are increasing their load. Our minds are already being overwhelmed with information, why load it with even more?

One young guy told me proudly how he had just completed on his first deal and now owned a cashflowing property. I asked him what he was going to do next (either buy more properties or source deals was the answer I expected). His reply was 'trade on the stock market'. He found something that worked and so, instead of doing it again and being successful again, he was going to start another new business model!?

I certainly needed to let my mind focus totally on *one* task – finding cashflowing property deals that I could buy or source to other bespoke clients. In 2010, when I wrote my first book, my buying rate dropped to one property a month. In 2011, when I developed my training business, I bought five properties in seven months. I definitely shop for property at a better rate when I am single-minded about it!

I have identified a cashflowing model – all I need to do is repeat it. As soon as you find your model, do it again and again. You need to develop a deeper understanding and knowledge in your model to become an expert. That expertise will enable you to reach your goal either by leveraging your money or by helping you to leverage other people's money for a fee. To change business models before you become financially secure seems like madness to me.

I do recognise that some people buy their first property and then realise that they don't enjoy it. If this is the case, I would suggest that you suffer for another year or two and build a portfolio that creates the financial secure platform from which you can develop any business and create any life you like. This is why your 'why' needs to be so powerful and compelling to help you stay focused.

I will say that it is no different if you are Sir Richard Branson, Warren Buffet or Lord Alan Sugar. Why? Because, although they now have massive teams of people to support them, they all started out on their own, focused on their own personal cash-creating strategy.

Yes, people like Robert Kiyosaki have interests in oil, gold, silver, property and businesses. Together with his wife, he started out investing in property and then built the Rich Dad Company once they had the financial security (the foundations) from which to diversify. Diversification is a good thing once you have achieved financial freedom. Once you have the money, time, knowledge, systems and team to support you, then you can diversify.

A key part in my ability to achieve the level of focus needed to be successful was having a coach. Even though I had created a powerful 'why', a powerful and compelling vision of my dream life, I still needed support – a trainer to guide me on my path. I jokingly have described myself as having obsessive compulsive disorder (OCD) combined with attention deficit disorder (ADD), in that I was completely focused on my goal and the tasks in hand until some shining opportunity caught my attention (mostly MLM businesses) and distracted me.

What shining possibility is taking your attention off your goal? What is delaying your journey to financial freedom?

Who is holding you accountable and helping you maintain the focus you need? If you are resisting this question, then you are not focused now and I bet you are not financially free either!

Case study – sometimes what you focus on is not what you want

For over a year, one of my client's efforts and attention were on property investment. For various technical reasons, the strategy was not working and the deserved success was not forthcoming. My client was working diligently 30 hours a week and was very successful to a point, but never quite closed the deal. Months later, it became clear that they were not following their passion. Their passion was to help others. This was their core value. They have now established a successful and inspiring coaching practice.

Case study – sometimes what you focus on is what you want; you just don't realise it

Four weeks into our coaching programme there was still resistance and a lack of results for one man with a clear vision of why he wanted to invest in property. He saw sourcing as the business model he could use to enhance his capital pot. Then came the breakthrough. The client realised that they wanted to pursue property through a different strategy – they really felt they wanted to buy and sell property as they had a limiting belief about the size of their capital pot and ability to attract funding. Their focus shifted and everything fell into line. They are now in the process of completing on their first deal. The real irony is that having achieved their first deal they can see how easy it is – they are now in the process of developing a sourcing business again and have attracted other private investors.

Coaching – what's good what's bad?

Committing to a coaching programme is an essential business need. Finding the right coach is the difference between success and a longer path! As with training courses, carry out a skills analysis – think about what you want to achieve. What skills do you need to be successful? What do you *honestly* have and what do you need help with? Who is successful in your industry? What is their story? When and how did they start? Be careful if they built their fortune using remortgaging, NMD or Mortgage Express-type strategies, as they may not have the relevant experience to help someone who is starting in a more conservative lending market.

When you identify the right person for you, make sure each session has a purpose, topic or challenge that needs resolving and discussing. It is all too easy to spend your time chatting or, worse, moaning. Make sure there is a structure to your sessions – ask about this upfront. Is this the structure that you want? Will it help you to achieve your goals?

Don't be afraid to end your sessions and choose another coach. This doesn't have to be because the first coach failed – hopefully it is because you outgrew them. When I work with a client, my aim is to make myself redundant. Then I know I have done a good job.

Have different coaches for different things. I have a coach who helps me with the personal challenges that come up in my life, especially apprehension when I reach each new entrepreneurial edge and I am about to take a massive step to change my business. I also have coaches who I use for sales training, property knowledge and business coaching. Look around – ask people and then get a coach.

Money matters

If this whole chapter is about making the transition from theory into real world business decisions, then money clearly matters and understanding how to use it as a tool is vital. Take credit cards – if you are going to use credit cards, you must understand the difference between good debt and bad debt, interest rates and of course leverage. I explain more about what lenders want in the financial section on pages 79–80. Right now, let's look at leverage using credit cards.

You can use a credit card to buy something you want – this could even be a property – and then pay off the credit card debt through monthly instalments. If you haven't mastered the proper technique, you will be paying interest on that debt, which will take you a lot longer to clear and be more expensive than a mortgage.

Alternatively, you can get a credit card offer for a balance transfer at 0%. (This usually comes with a 3% fee but over a year this is still cheap money.) Depending on the lender, this can be spent or transferred into a bank account. Imagine if you could get £20,000 spread over two or three credit cards all at 0% and then use that money to fund a property purchase. The property could give you £200–£250 per month net cashflow, which would pay off the monthly credit card costs. Then, in a year's time, remortgage the property, release the equity (which may or may not equal the credit card bill) and clear the card (or refinance at 0% again if you have to). Now the property will give more cashflow. None of this was your money – you leveraged available resources.

Are you a homeowner with a 'drawdown mortgage facility'? This is an agreement that you can borrow money against the value of your house when you need it and repay it without penalty. Examples of this include some Woolwich mortgages, First Direct, Virgin or Halifax One accounts.

If you have sufficient equity, you can 'draw down' or borrow against your home, buy an investment property, refurbish, remortgage and repay the money back to your mortgage account. You will have then bought a property with none of your own money all totally legally. You could have £200–£300 extra cashflow per month. What if you keep repeating this process? These are some of the strategies I discuss in my first book, *Using Other People's Money*.

If you are going to start using money (other people's money), then you must understand interest and ROI. ROI or cash-on-cash returns is a way of measuring just how much the money you are using is earning. This can be compared to banks' interest rates or the costs of borrowing the original capital sums.

The formula is simple:

- Above the dividing line is the net profit from the investment. So, in the example of buying a buy-to-let property, above the line is the annual net rent. This is the gross rent from the tenant minus the letting agent fees, the mortgage and, I believe, the property insurance, because without paying the mortgage or the property insurance you can't have the money to buy the house in the first place.

- Below the dividing line are all the cash costs needed to get the property to a point where it produces rent. So the deposit on the property (20–25%), the solicitor, surveyor and broker fees, costs to refurbish the property, gas certificates, tenant search fees (without which you wouldn't have a tenant to pay rent) and, when sourcing for a bespoke client, my sourcing fee (which is another cost incurred when buying the property because without my help you would not have that specific deal).

- When you divide the smaller top number by the larger bottom number you will get a figure less than one. Maybe 0.10 or anything from 0.04–0.35 – this is effectively a percentage (10, 4 or 35%). This means that this investment would earn you that percentage income, and so you can compare that to the less risky interest offered by the savings accounts or the cost of borrowing the money to fund the investment. More examples are worked out for you in Chapter 8 from page 131 onwards.

You can use this information to calculate potential profit shares or payments to joint venture partners. This is a much more realistic measure to calculate the difference between two investment opportunities as it includes all costs, rather than yield which only divides gross rent by actual purchase price.

The last thing to consider is to never give up the day job! Without a regular salary, you will not be able to get a mortgage and then all of this is mute. Someone in your investment team – your husband, girlfriend or brother – has to work and earn a sufficient salary to meet the lenders' criteria. For example, some lenders want you to earn over £24,000 per annum as a second surety against the rent not coming in. Money matters – know where yours is coming from, how much it costs and what it will earn you!

Time matters

Once you take on an entrepreneurial spirit and lifestyle, the old nine-to-five mentality seems strange, unnatural even. You become passionate and enthusiastic about what you are doing – something lots of employees fail to experience. Unfortunately, what also happens is that you forget to value your time!

I think this is what makes me most frustrated when I speak to other investors or to clients. They can talk about all the things they are doing to find a deal, the adverts, the number of clever marketing activities, the conversations with 'potential vendors' (especially those doing lease options). Yet, when they talk about the 'returns' they are making, the deals they are transacting, they are spending lots of time for very little cash return. Some are earning less than the £2.50 I achieved through MLM – that doesn't motivate me.

My question is how many hours of work do you need to put into a strategy before you have a cast-iron deal that will generate cashflow? If you have a brilliant system that filters out those 'potential' deals and leaves you working on live deals that conclude within 4–8 weeks, then great. Most option strategy followers spend up to a year getting their first deal and that's after they have spent a year 'having a go' at below market valuation (BMV) or some other strategy.

The principle is simple. How much time did you spend to earn how much money? What is the return on your time invested (ROTI) in the deal – cash for time cost? Then, divide one into the other and you have your hourly rate. I worked this out with one client and they spent a year earning £200 per month. Yes, I know there are back end 'potential' pay outs when in three, five or seven years you finalise the deal (*if* you can, *if* the economic situation and *if* the lending situation enables it). Meantime, you still have to eat, pay your home costs and your utility bills.

When the strategy you are following does not tie in with your financial goals and provide the income stream you need quickly, then how can you sustain that strategy without moving into debt? (Unless, of course, you planned to have a whole year's income in your cashflow account to support yourself during this time!) The key to success in property in my opinion is answering the question: how can you make money from your property knowledge as quickly as possible? You will need to be congruent and ethical to have a long-term, stress-free future. You will need to work hard!

If you were to source one deal for a £2,000 fee once a month, would that help? What about one deal at £5,000 every other month? Could you scale that up once you had your system worked out?

Cash rich or cash poor?

Now what if you were to start again and make money this time? How much money would you need a month to cover expenses? How much would you need to become financially secure – or even financially free?

The crucial place to start is with your income and expenses. If expenses exceed income, then you are in trouble straight away – even if it is just by £250 per month that's £3,000 debt after one year. When I first took a look at our income and expenses (we were still working but I was being made redundant – so I thought I would check), we were doing okay. What I noticed was how many old insurance policies we had, medical cover, life, etc. and then subscriptions for magazines we had no time to read!

I checked our new insurance requirements and the paperwork carefully and then cancelled everything unnecessary and unused. What are you paying for that is unnecessary? If your expenses exceed your income, you might need to move beyond looking at just the direct debits in your bank account and look at your actual spending habits. I have a spreadsheet that I share with clients to help them record all of their spending (available at TheSourcersApprentice. com). Complete this, or a similar, spreadsheet for a month – for the whole family – and see what you are spending your money on.

I heard a brilliant explanation of people's spending habits. Robert Kiyosaki said that your expenses are like a forecast on your future: 'What you spend on now is what you will get in the future.' If you spend your money on coaching, personal development and wealth creation, then you will get wealthy. If you spend your money on shoes, you will get a packed wardrobe. If you spend your money on take-away meals and computer games, you will get a big a_ _ _! (I leave you to fill in the blanks.)

The temptation is to spiral into blame and argument, especially if money is a stressor in your house (either for you alone or for your family). Remember, money is a resource that needs managing, monitoring and, above all, leveraging!

Once you know whether you are in equilibrium or in debt, then you can start to make informed decisions.

How much are you worth?

Even without the information from the family budget spreadsheet, you can still work out how much you are worth. However, I believe that you need all of the information and you can draft these figures now and then use the spreadsheet to confirm or amend your true spending habits.

Once you know your monthly outgoings, you know the baseline figure that you need to generate in order to meet expenses. Let's assume £2,500 is the baseline figure, as this will cover the outgoings that the majority of families experience (please do use your own figures if you prefer). Please note that I am not going to work out tax, etc. Let's just keep the numbers simple for the purposes of this exercise. £2,500 per month means £30,000 per annum (2500 x 12).

Now, as a professional investor, you can't just decide to earn £2,500 per month – that is not enough detail to be sure that you can really focus on what you need to be doing. So let's break that down into how you spend your time.

I believe we can use four categories (I love it when things are in fours – it's neat and geometrical). They are as follows:

1. Income generating time – time that you can actually send someone an invoice for.
2. Income speculating time – time spent networking for a client or speaking with a live and interested vendor.
3. Income saving time – time spent on accounts and property maintenance. It is just as important to keep your money once you have it as it is to acquire it in the first place.
4. Other – this includes everything from personal development, family and fitness, to reading a book, or anything you want to do that does not fall into the first three core categories – life!

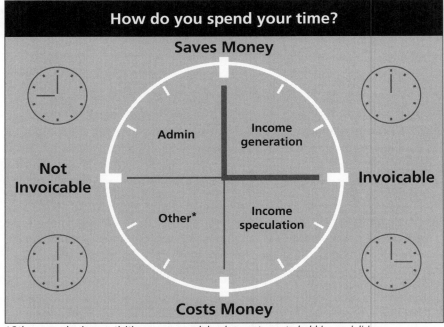

How do you spend your time?

Saves Money

Admin

Income generation

Not Invoicable

Invoicable

Other*

Income speculation

Costs Money

Other – non-business activities, eg. personal development, sports, hobbies, socialising.

Again, you can keep a record over a month and see how you spend your time. Right now, by writing this book, I am spending a lot of time on income speculating activity. This is because, although I will sell this book in the future (you are reading it after all), I cannot send an invoice to anyone while I am writing it.

How you spend your time is very relevant to your cashflow position because if you are expenses-high and income-poor, then you have to spend more time generating income than anything else. If you are at equilibrium (where income equals expenses), then you can think about growing your business to the next level – to generate more income – and so spend some time on income speculation activities.

How much does an hour cost?

The next step is to calculate your hourly rate. Given that you will spend only a portion of your time actually invoicing for income, you can imagine that you will not have an hourly rate in the same way an employee has one (based on just showing up at their place of work) – that simply is not enough now!

Let's say that out of the 52 weeks of the year you will work for 48 weeks – you will need time off to recharge your batteries, see family and have the odd bank holiday. If you are still in a very active learning phase and part of a programme around property, personal development or on a mentorship, you will need to add in time to allow you to complete these activities too.

Now out of the 48 weeks (roughly 11 months) you will not work weekends (in an ideal world – of course in reality you might) and you will aim to work Monday to Friday for about eight hours per day (nine to five). You can reduce this if you are planning to work part time.

So, depending on what you offer to clients, in whatever form that takes, you will have chargeable time. In my case (so you can see how this works), let's say in one week I could source a property for a client, offer a three-hour strategy session and also coach people one-to-one or teach them in a group.

Next let's think about how much time I can invoice for. This is looking at it in one direction – we will come back and check feasibility in a minute. Well, I estimate I can source one property a week, have one strategy session and then five coaching clients. Okay, how many hours will that take?

- Sourcing a property from start to finish = 8 days.

- Strategy session = 3 hours.

- Coaching = 5 x 1 hour.

Well, the above clearly doesn't work as the total comes to more hours than there are in a week – nine days in fact. That's two more days than available on any of the calendars I know.

Let's be more realistic and reverse the process. Let's estimate one property to be sourced per month (eight days), one strategy session per month (three hours) and one coaching client per month (four hours). So that is a rough total of nine invoice days per month.

Now my target earnings were £30,000 per year and I have 11 months of working time – so that is £2,727 per month. When divided by my nine potential invoice days, that gives a daily rate of £303 per day. If I can invoice for seven hours per day, then I could charge £43.28 per hour.

The reality of this exercise is that you will need more than £30,000 to cover the expenses of running your business. You will need to pay for travel, marketing, advertising, membership to certain professional bodies and certain training courses – you will also need a coach.

The £30,000 will need to be **net profit** from your business. Depending on what services you offer clients, how you find them and distances you have to travel, then you will have to double or even triple the £30,000 target to generate that level of profit. So, in reality, your daily rate to earn £30,000 per year needs to be approximately £80–£130 per hour if you are only going to invoice nine days a month. You could, of course, work more days a month…

You can start to see that you can move these figures around. Let's say you want a turnover of £90,000 to give at least £30,000 clear profit.

£90,000 / 11 months = £8,182 per month (approximately).

Let's say you invoice for 10 days per month. This means you need to charge £818 per day. So, if it takes eight days work to identify, source, manage and tenant a property for a client, then you need to charge £6,544.

Do it at home – do it at work

As with your household, you will need to monitor the business expenses as well as the business income. In the first year or two it will cost more, as you may set up a website, or make mistakes on advertising or in other areas. You may also have a higher learning cost as a percentage than in later years.

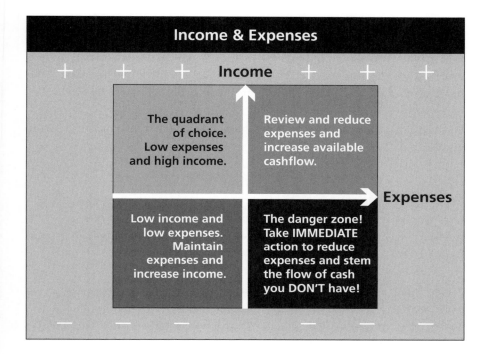

I hope this helps you to understand the following key concepts:

1. Know what is happening with your income and expenses – track them and make corrections so that you get back to at least equilibrium as soon as possible.
2. Know what you need to earn a year to calculate your hourly rate – remember to cover the business expenses as well as the household expenses.
3. Make sure your strategy pays. Go back and look at how much time you spend to get a cashflowing deal and work out your hourly rate. If it takes a year to get one deal at £200 per month, then 200 x 12 is £2,400 per annum. If you are working 11 months, 20 days per month, seven hours a day, then your hourly rate will be £1.56!

The game of consequences

I remember hearing the phrase: 'Every decision has a consequence – evaluate the consequences upfront!' and I love it. Sometimes we make rash decisions and they work out, other times they don't. Sometimes we don't make a decision and nothing changes. Sometimes everything goes wrong. Personally, I prefer to make decisions, take action and influence the shape of my life.

I have had a few philosophical debates over recent months about people believing their life is preordained and therefore they don't need to worry as 'what will be will be'. I don't think it is a question of preordained, predetermined or self-created – the question is one of involvement and participation. There is a joke:

A man found himself the sole survivor of a shipwreck and as he prayed to God in the water he asked to be saved: 'Please God save me.' A little while later, a large piece of wreckage passed by floating on the surface and the man ignored it as he continued to pray: 'Please God save me.' After an hour, a boat passed by and he ignored it and continued to pray: 'Please God save me.' As the day grew on and the man grew weary, a plane flew over the site of the boat's last-known sighting; it circled and left as the man continued to pray: 'Please God save me.' Finally, exhausted, the man could no longer tread water and drowned. As he arrived at the gates of Heaven, the man asked St Peter, 'What happened? I prayed and prayed to be saved. Why didn't God save me?' St Peter said, 'He sent a piece of wreckage, a boat and a plane – what more did you want?'

The point I hope I have made is, no matter what your beliefs are, you need to play your role in your life to achieve the outcomes you want, or are destined to have. What choices or decisions are you making and have you evaluated them?

Consequences

- If you give up work or don't manage your credit score, you will not be able to get a mortgage in your own name.

- If you don't understand the value of your time and the time cost of your chosen strategy, you will run out of money as your expenses exceed your income.

- If you don't have a clear strategy of how to make money from your property knowledge, you will not create the cashflow you need to sustain your lifestyle, even as it is now.

- If you are not clear about your focus, you will flit from one strategy to another and from one deal to another until you fail.

- If you don't know why you want to do this or what you expect from property, then what will keep you going when you face the challenges we all must face? Why will you succeed when others fail? What will make you successful?

What are the consequences of the decisions you are making (or not making)?

- On-going debt.
- Increasing debt.
- No mortgages.
- No cashflowing deals.
- No income.
- No success.
- Failure, disappointment and resignation as you return to a job to make ends meet in a worse situation than when you left work.

So the actions you need to take now are simple:

- First, record and monitor your time and work out how much time certain key activities take you.

- Second, monitor your expenses – understand if you are income-rich or expenses-poor.

This will give you the outline of your personal financial strategy:

- You will understand whether or not you can 'afford' to follow a certain investment strategy.
- You will be able to take immediate and decisive action to ensure that your finances are at least at a point of equilibrium.
- You can make informed decisions about the 'services' you can offer and what they will cost (see Section 3, Chapter 9, page 139).
- You know how much your time is worth and can choose to spend it differently – is four hours in front of the TV worth the lost £400 of potential income you could have earned?

Moving on to the money

Section 1 covers the critical skills that I recognised in other successful entrepreneurs and decided to discover, develop or enhance for my own purpose, to become independently wealthy and financially free.

Why reinvent the wheel? If you see people achieving the goals and business success you want, then work out what it is that they know and understand that you don't. Then learn and understand it for yourself.

I started with this type of knowledge as I believe that all successful and long-lasting business people have developed the skills to master their own minds before they start mastering money. That's the difference between a wealthy future and a lottery winner lifestyle. Successful people understand that self-belief, focus and action get results.

Now that your mind is mastered and you understand 'why' you want to invest in property and have a property business, rather than just remain an investor, it's time to move on to mastering the money. Understanding the financial markets and how money flows is critical in business and even more so in property investment. Successful people understand that it is the relative value of money and the skill in leveraging that money that creates long-lasting wealth.

Section 2

Understanding the economic environment

Chapter 4

The business of investing

You need to shift your thinking from an investor mindset (looking for houses and cash) to a business mindset – a more entrepreneurial way of thinking. When you start to think about serving markets, consumer needs and supply and demand, the result will be a shift in business growth.

- Do you understand the tax, mindset and business benefits of being an investor or business owner rather than an employee?

- Have you read Robert Kiyosaki? Which books have you read?

- Do you think of money as real money, or recognise its relative worth and leverage potential?

This chapter will take you through the fundamental economic lessons I have picked up – in a simple-to-understand way:

- Seize opportunities to become financially free.

- Education – where to look.

- Strategy – how to pick the right one.

- Leverage other people's money.

- What's your offer?

- Do you know your value?

- Have you got the right team and can you lead them?

Nothing is the same: B and I > E and S

Whether you have given up work or plan to, have savings and equity to invest or are borrowing money, you must protect your financial future by understanding what is going on in the market and how it *will* affect you. Anything else and you really are gambling with your future, and that is definitely *not* what I am about.

This book is all about changing your mindset and business model from investor to business owner. In the previous chapters, I have discussed the mental skills and concepts I believe are vital to success. What I haven't done yet, is explain why and how to make that step change to become a business owner.

Once again, if you haven't read Kiyosaki or been shown his four quadrant concept (E, S, B, I), then I urge you to pause, if only to check it out online.

In summary, the benefit of moving to the right side of Kiyosaki's quadrant is that business owners and investors pay tax differently. Effectively, as an employee, you earn, pay tax and then spend what's left. As a business owner, you earn, spend and get taxed on what's left. Now legitimate tax deductions need to be checked with your accountant or tax advisor, but, put simply, the cost of travel, phone, internet and possibly accommodation associated with the direct purchase of an investment property can be paid from pre-tax profit.

Why is this important?

Employee		Business owner or investor	
Earns	£1,000	Earns	£1,000
Tax @ 35% including National Insurance	-£350	Expenses including phone, travel and internet	-£270
Take home pay	£650	Profit liable for tax	£730
Cost of phone, travel and internet	-£270	Tax @ 35%	-£255.50
What's left?	£380	What's left?	£474.50

Depending on the business model, expenses could be considerably higher.

Tax benefits are just one reason to think like a business owner. I believe the real benefit of being a business owner is the acknowledgement that you are taking active responsibility for your financial future and all that entails.

Remember, I explained that every decision has a consequence. Just evaluate it upfront. If this section or topic is stressful, perhaps because you feel you don't understand it, then learn it. Without being rude, it is that simple. I sat in a class at school where the teacher spoke about economics and I stared out of the window! Now I know how vital it is – a core business skill that you need to learn and keep updated. It can be as simple as reading the *Financial Times*, the business and financial sections of *The Times* or *The Guardian*, checking the BBC or Sky News websites for stories – or change who you talk to – who you listen to.

Go where the conversations are happening! That, in part, is why I belong to Ecademy – because of the variety and degree of business knowledge and the level and variety of the conversations. Did you go to Excel in July 2011 to listen to Lord Alan Sugar and Sir Richard Branson? What about the Business Show in 2012? If not, why not? You need to know this stuff. Okay, enough nagging!

My economic and business mentors

Apart from the greats, like Branson and Sugar, there is one reliable and easily accessible source of forward-thinking economic and business knowledge and that is Robert Kiyosaki, author of *Rich Dad Poor Dad* (1997) and, more recently, *Rich Dad's Conspiracy of the Rich: The 8 New Rules of Money* (2010) and *An Unfair Advantage: The Power of Financial Education* (2011).

Opportunities to hear people like Branson, Sugar and Kiyosaki speak are possible but rare. There are a great many other brilliant thinkers and speakers about business, money flows and the economy; if you get an opportunity, go along and listen. Through my connection with Ecademy and Daniel Priestley, founder of Triumphant Events, I have been fortunate enough to hear Darren Shirlaw speak about his attitude to business, money, the economy and much more.

Darren Shirlaw is, for me, like an English (or perhaps I should say Australian) Kiyosaki with his own twist and flavour. His attention is on creating and building successful businesses. He declares himself a 'boring mathematician' – he is far from that – more an entrepreneur and business genius. Some key lessons from Shirlaw include:

- Focus in the form of sticking to one business idea and pursuing it to success;

- Economic lifecycle – not in terms of boom and bust, but in terms of business era – defining business drive;

- Intention – or, as I would say, 'Why?' What is your passion?; and

- Money – how we use it over family generations – what it means to us, and how to leverage it.

Kiyosaki has dramatically influenced the direction of my understanding and my wider financial plans due to reading (or listening to) his books. It can get complicated when he talks about 401ks, but that is why playing his CashFlow game has really helped me to put his key lessons into practice.

- Know the difference between assets and liabilities.

- Understand how money flows.

- Don't put all of your faith in the government or education system – they want you to have a job and pay taxes.

- Get a financial education so you understand money.

Lord Alan Sugar (the grand-daddy of business), TV portrayal aside, understands the core fundamentals of business – how to buy, sell, market and invest. Above all, his defining question to my ears was, 'Where is the money? If the business is not going to make money in the first few months, it's not a business.'

Sir Richard Branson inspires everyone to 'follow your heart, find your passion, make a difference' and 'just do it'. Behind all the passion and media attention is an incredible businessman who, like Lord Sugar, inspires and leads a fantastic team of business brains without whose support none of his success would be possible. Leadership is vital to business success – more so than passion. Without leadership no decisions are made. An entrepreneur leverages money, resources and labour to create success and that takes leadership.

I am going to cover in brief a few of these economic lessons. You may start to see a pattern and almost a repetition as these messages come from so many different sources. So, let's start by putting these overlapping lessons in some form of order – not out of preference or importance, just for the sake of structure.

Focus and intention

The message here seems to be the usual – focus on one thing until successful and *then* you can diversify. The underlying point is that there is a time lag (and a series of skills) needed to be successful in a chosen field. Too many small businesses bump along just making ends meet, as they repeatedly switch business focus – for example, property to stocks to MLM, or property to coaching to internet! Even within the field of coaching be clear – become an expert and let your clients and market know who and what you stand for.

Kiyosaki clearly admits that, while he has learnt and explored various asset classes, he knows where his passion lies and he knows what he is good at and so that is what he focuses on. However, he built his financial security first – then diversified.

This is where I use the word 'why?' Shirlaw speaks of intention, others use words like purpose or passion. It can become really overwhelming for people with certain personality types to think about what their passion is – they don't feel that 'passionate' and that's okay. Yet we often know 'why' we want to do something or what we want our business to result in; we know what our intention is by starting a business venture.

If you can't articulate 'why' at the moment, then make it a priority to draw this out and develop it. It is not a static thing. It is okay to evolve your future the more you experience, the more you can imagine. Tom Evans has written a brilliant e-book that discusses how to set goals in terms of learning rather than having or doing. He comments that you will be stifled by the limitations of what you can imagine now – whereas your thoughts can be expanded by imagining what you could learn. Find a copy at TheSourcersApprentice.com.

The business message here is: start your business idea with the end in mind. How much do you want to earn? What do you want to do? What do you want to have? How do you want to work on a day-to-day basis? What is your exit strategy? What will you have created? What will you leave behind?

Economic lifecycle

This is fascinating and I am sure common knowledge to some people. This is not the usual economic cycle of boom and bust, or even the interesting perspective given by Dr Rohan Weerasinghe about the the baby boomers, their children and the impact of their associates' spending habits as they pass through the economic cycle.

This is about the 'eras of business' – the developments and fundamental shifts in corporate thinking.

For example:

- 1950s–60s was the production era – a bubble of innovation and productivity in post-war England. Then as we hit the late 1960s, it was hard to differentiate one product from another, so

- 1970s–80s became the image era – remember the Marlborough Man?

- By 1990, the world was swamped with images. Now we needed companies to position themselves, place themselves in the mind of the client with a message that said why they were different. We became more time conscious and looked for the perfect pitch that spoke directly to us and our individual needs.

- In 2000, the web became more mainstream and companies identified it as a new marketing channel, and so it became the distribution era.

Shirlaw explains that small businesses follow the trend about 10 years behind that of large corporate shifts. This means that 2010 onwards is the dawn of the distribution era for small businesses as more than 50% of sales move to the web. While small businesses are focused on developing online sales, the corporates have moved back round the cycle to production, as they need new products that just use the online medium, for example Kindle and iphones.

Dr Rohan Weerasinghe talks about the impact that human generational-spending (my word) has had and continues to have on the economy. I see this as similar to the Shirlaw concept of eras of business – eras of human generation. The culture, buying and spending habits of each generation impact on the economy and how the money flows. For example, a generation of spenders takes money from wages and spends it in the economy; a generation of savers puts their money in the bank rather than directly into circulation.

The bulges of population caused by the baby boomers and now their children are sweeping through the economy, as a large percentage of the population all reach an age of consumer demand at the same time – they all have children so sales in baby-related products soar. The children of the baby boomer generation are starting to leave home with the impact that family homes are now too big for their needs. The baby boomers spend on their children until they leave home and then all their focus shifts to their savings. They are starting to downsize towards retirement.

The younger generation are leaving university with mountains of debt and need to move out into the real world away from parents. Mostly, they will have to move into the rental market as the combination of debt and lack of savings means they do not have the means to buy their own home. As they start to join the employment market there could be a rise in their disposable income. This spending bulge will arrive as their parents reduce their spending in response to forthcoming retirement. The popularity of consumable products will swing from those items attractive to the 50+ age group to those favoured by educated and technologically aware 20-somethings.

What if you could get ahead of the small business curve by emulating big business? What could you do to increase your business through the product concept? I know you are a property investor but you still need to understand the web and, more importantly, social media. You could still produce e-books or reports for clients. That is why in early 2011, as a business, I decided to learn about online marketing and what it means to take a business 'digital'. I, along with my business partner, now offer this knowledge to our clients through a strategic business planning process.

There has to be a reason to go digital – you need a business purpose. There is no point 'tweeting' to thousands of people if you cannot convert those conversations to sales. That is why property businesses will have products and services to sell to clients at all levels of the sales chain; from high-value face-to-face services through to lower-cost replicable products or services.

What do you need to learn? Who do you need to talk with to understand the digital medium as a communication channel and maximise your opportunity to transact business through the web?

Get a financial education – asset, liabilities and cashflow

We all went to school, theoretically, to get a good education. In fact, we were trained. The term 'education' comes from the Latin meaning to 'pull out' or 'draw out'. Do you feel that your internal knowledge was pulled out, that it flowed from you? Or did you sit there and recite the alphabet and times table, like me?

I have written earlier in the Introduction to this book about the difference between education, understanding and training – it is the difference between having the information but not the knowledge and understanding to apply it. Take algebra as a case in point.

The British education system does not prepare young people, I would argue, for life or the world of work. Young people are not taught about assets and liabilities, about income and expenses. They might, depending on their choices at A Level, do some basic accounts as part of a business course, but there is no context or linking back to the real lives ahead of them. Why? Because the system needs them to be employees!

If you have children, the greatest gifts you can give them are, first, the game of Monopoly, then move on to CashFlow and buy them Kiyosaki's books for children. They were, after all, born to keep you in the style you would like your old age to be – luxurious. So you'd better give them the education to manage their money and invest it wisely in property and not the building society or designer clothes!

Money – how it flows, is used and is leveraged

Earlier, I covered leverage and ROI in a lot of detail; understanding these concepts is vital for success. If you do not understand how money moves and what it costs, how can you access it and afford to pay to borrow it?

Shirlaw talks about the concepts of 'relative money' and 'real money'. The poor think about and deal with real money – that is the pound coins and five pound notes in their wallets. They try to acquire it and then they want to hold on to it. They do not understand the relative value of money. They don't understand the power and value of leverage.

The rich and super rich understand about the relative value of money and you do too! Money is a resource that can be used and leveraged to create more money. Understanding money is a continuum: at one end, people with no idea and no money; at the other end, people grasping and holding tightly to the small amounts they do possess, in fear of losing what they have. If you recognise money as a resource to be used, then you reside in the middle with the rich and super rich.

What are your thoughts about money?

Underlying this understanding about money is the concept of abundance. This can apply to so many areas of your life. I know without a shadow of a doubt that you are one of the top 10% richest people in the world – simply because you are here in Europe and reading this book. Do you feel abundant? It depends what you use as a comparison, of course. The truth is you are rich

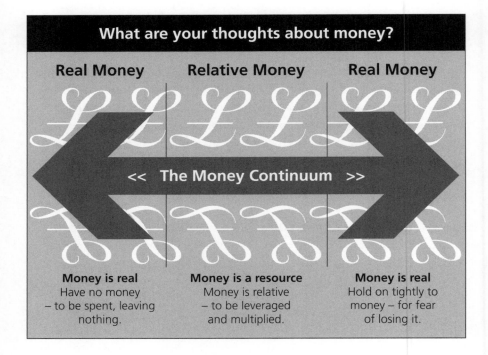

What are your thoughts about money?

Real Money	Relative Money	Real Money
<<	The Money Continuum	>>
Money is real	**Money is a resource**	**Money is real**
Have no money – to be spent, leaving nothing.	Money is relative – to be leveraged and multiplied.	Hold on tightly to money – for fear of losing it.

in so many ways – revel in that feeling for a while. If you don't understand this concept, again, I recommend that you read Christopher Howard's book *Turning Passions into Profits* mentioned in Section 1.

Let's think about water. Is water abundant? You know where to find it and how to gather it when you need to use it, mostly because we are spoilt by taps and Perrier. Yet, if you were about to cross the desert, would you learn even more about water – that precious life-preserving resource? That is what money is – a precious resource. You need to learn about where to find it and how and when to use it.

To explain leveraging a business and business capacity, Shirlaw uses the same metaphor of 'context' and 'content' that Kiyosaki uses to explain knowledge. In Shirlaw's metaphor the context is a glass and the content is water. If the glass is full (either your head with knowledge and ideas or your business with sales), then you cannot grow until you tip out some of the water to let more flow in or get a bigger glass. Let's get a bigger glass and pour all the water (or business) from the first glass into the larger second glass. What happens is that you have more space in the second glass to add more water (business sales or knowledge).

In this model, the crucial figures are between 40–80% capacity. If your business sales and cashflow reside between these figures, great, as long as that is enough cash to meet the life of your dreams. If your business for whatever reason is producing less than 40% of your potential sales income or using less than 40% of your total sales opportunity time, then you will have a lower cashflow, and even cashflow issues.

Alternatively, if your business is operating at 80% capacity or above, then I guarantee you are stressed. You need to develop systems, outsource and/or grow your business. You need to expand your business into a bigger model or a larger glass.

I mentioned in Chapter 3 on page 51 about valuing your time and working out what you are worth. I said that you had four ways of using your time: income generating; income speculating; income saving; and 'other'. If you now apply this level of understanding to the concept above, you need to make sure that your business invoices or generates income for 80% of the month – that means 24 days.

Remember the example I showed when we were calculating your hourly rate? If you only work (invoice and earn money) for 10 days a month, then you are only working at 30% capacity. Why? Because you could be earning money for 30 days per month if you developed the systems, products and services to meet your client's needs. If you invoiced £800 a day for 365 days a year, that would be £292,000 before costs and tax. If you get the systems right that is not going to be the same as 'working' for 365 days of your life!

How is this possible if you have to spend time speculating, saving and living your life? Because you outsource the capacity and that is how your business grows. An easy example is to use a letting agent – trade 10% of your rent for their time. They will manage the property, the tenant and the repairs and you use the time to source more properties and generate more income. Another example is to use trades people to refurbish your property rather than doing it yourself. They are quicker (guaranteed because they do it all the time), more professional (ditto) and your time is more valuably spent sourcing other deals.

Leadership

So this brings us to leadership and the examples set by Sugar (the real man not the TV caricature) and Branson. They have different styles that we may never truly understand until we experience it personally, but what they have in common is a clear vision – expertly communicated to all of their staff. Both are passionate men – they just have different styles and personalities. Their staff are well treated, kept informed and very loyal. Sugar and Branson understand the vision and purpose of their businesses, communicating them clearly to the staff team and encouraging their buy-in, support and contribution. These have to be traits of leadership.

There are so many books on leadership; it would be impractical to list them here. However, one book I particularly like is John C. Maxwell's *The 21 Irrefutable Laws of Leadership* (1998). Maxwell uses quotes and stories to explain the vital concepts that any great leader must understand. The examples of leadership and inspiring words bring the concepts home in a way that pure theory fails to do.

How to apply this and become a business owner

Instead of being a property investor who buys houses and gets stuck when there is no more money, I believe that if you think like and become a property business owner with all the concepts talked about so far, then you will grow your business and your portfolio quicker and more easily than many others. You'll also pay less tax in the process!

There are two selling points for me:

1. You can start thinking in terms of products and services and that is more creative than just houses.
2. You can start to leverage your time, money and, more importantly, other people's time and money, and all by taking active responsibility.

Think about products and services for a minute – how is this different from thinking about houses? I recognised that my tenant was actually a customer who I was selling to. I was selling them the idea that they wanted to live in my property and that they wanted to stay there for a long time. Then I thought about the vendor – what service could I offer them? Then my estate agent, and so on. It has changed the way I do business and has opened up lots of opportunities that I have put into practice.

I also thought about what I had to offer – what do people who I meet want from me? In January 2010, I spoke at the two January Berkshire Property Meetings for just five to seven minutes before Dr Rohan Weerasinghe took to the stage as the main speaker. Afterwards, I was surrounded by people asking questions and I soon realised that people wanted to know what I had been doing. So I wrote a book. I saw the book as a way to use my time effectively – write once, share many times. Now I had my first product.

This time I have written a book using a better more professional, cost-effective and time-effective system. This book will generate more profit than the first book because I have employed a great team, the strategy was planned from the start and the marketing is better – I recognise this is a product. The third book will do even better as I apply the new lessons I am learning, and so on.

Finally, in 2011, I took the very challenging step (for me as a committed control freak) to outsource some of my business. Even as I write, I can think of more tasks that I want to hand over to my virtual assistant (VA). I understand that VAs can be sourced on the web – there are plenty of sites depending on what skills you need. However, I preferred to meet and get to know the person who was going to access my files and websites. I needed to 'see' someone to trust them – old fashioned and unnecessary and something that definitely slowed me down. Having said this, I know plenty of investors who are landlords because they don't trust a letting agent! I am now in the process of creating a replicable system that other investors can follow – complete with 'how to' and 'what if' instructions – another new product.

So, why be a business owner? Because you can leverage other people's time and money to grow your property portfolio quicker and more easily. *Why do that?* So that you can be financially secure and start enjoying the financial freedom and lifestyle that you want.

Is this compelling enough?

How do you become a business owner?

You need to take this knowledge and understanding and apply it to your own circumstances. You need to decide on your own repeatable and replicable model of property sourcing. You need to identify where your skills and experience lie, what your knowledge and passion is about. This will form the basis of your business model.

So just to repeat the steps:

1. Know why you want to invest in property. What do you expect to get out of it? What will the business look like? How much will you earn (do the maths)? How will you earn your cashflow?
2. Get financially educated; you have started by reading this book, now read Kiyosaki if you haven't already, and not just *Rich Dad, Poor Dad*. Read *Rich Dad's Conspiracy of the Rich: The 8 New Rules of Money* and *An Unfair Advantage: The Power of Financial Education*. Look at who you mix with – what groups you attend. Expand your network. Join something like Ecademy, which has online and offline capacity (unlike LinkedIn) but does not burden you with building other people's businesses like the BRN (Business Referral Network). Have conversations with your accountant, tax advisor and other business owners. Get a good broker who follows the market and can discuss the mood of the

Monetary Policy Committee with you. My accountant holds client briefing events to help us grow our businesses. Who can you connect with, talk to and listen to about all things financial and economic?

3. Pick the right strategy and know the other strategies that can be used if need be. Remember about the value of your time – make sure the strategy will pay you a decent 'wage' for your time, otherwise Tesco, Marks & Spencer or Boots is starting to look like a better option! Understand what you want to achieve financially and then give yourself the best possible chance of achieving it. My money 'is on' and comes from property sourcing. I am my own client and so my system is replicable. It is costed to make sure I earn a decent amount for my time (which is a valuable and limited resource – the only limited resource in reality!)

4. Leverage where possible – use other people's money and other people's time. You will need to understand the relative cost of money and ROI in order to explain the opportunity to potential clients. Outsource by using a letting agent, bookkeeper, accountant, builder and, if you can, a cleaner. Work these costings into your business model.

5. Understand what you have to offer your clients. What is your service? Why should they sell to you or buy or rent from you and not someone else? To do this you will need to understand what you know, what you have experience of, what your skills are and where your passion lies. It is one of the fundamental bits of personal analysis that we do with mentees, because if you can't explain to me why I should do business with you, then I will work with someone else who can. Then remember in this seemingly 'me-me' world that what you have to offer has to be all about 'them' and not about 'you'. To make that transition from understanding yourself to understanding your client market is crucial; so crucial that the success of your business will rest upon you achieving it. Know your client, picture them, know where to find them and always speak directly to them. Refine it over time – it will change. It has to be good, but it does not have to be perfect first time! Develop your niche and message accordingly.

6. Know your value. What are you selling and what is it worth? Recognise whether you are selling a replicable model (what you do) or the skills to act as an agent (not location or strategy specific).

7. Get the right team. I have already mentioned that you need to speak to the right people to increase your financial knowledge; you also need the right team to deliver a service to your clients. Know that you can trust the people you are building your business around. You don't need to use just one solicitor or even just one broker. A level of consistency will build trust and relationships, but you need to be prepared to change if their ability to meet your service needs doesn't come up to your expected standard or response times. Just a word of caution here – if you are only passing on one deal a quarter, you are probably not a top client – so build on your business and that relationship first.

In Section 3, I explain the practicalities and specifics of setting up a sourcing business and, of course, you can access the videos and audios that accompany this book on TheSourcersApprentice.com.

Continuous professional development and accountability

Continuing your training is crucial, but there is a balance to be had. I changed during 2010 from attending four to six property networks a month, plus three out of four weekends either attending or supporting property training courses because, quite simply, I wanted more of a personal life.

By going to fewer events, I had more time to think about what I wanted to get out of each event that I did attend. What was my intention for attending? If you can clearly articulate what you want to learn, then you can seek out the right teachers, mentors and coaches. If you can clearly articulate who you want to meet, then you can attend the right events and networks.

When it comes to coaching I have the following approach; I have the wonderful Johnnie Cass as my personal coach – we speak once a month – more if necessary – to ensure that I am focused on my goals and tackle the inevitable challenges of building a business head on. Alongside Johnnie, I have taken on a variety of business or skill-specific coaches for a period of time to acquire certain knowledge. For example, I spent time enhancing my sales skills, mastering website strategies, developing my books and other products, and business and product development, and so on.

So what if I just want to be a property investor?

Great, that's a brilliant choice because at least you have read the previous chapters in this book. You have had a chance to see the opportunity and decided that it is not right for you at this moment, unless of course you have an underlying negative belief.

What difference will it make? Maybe none. If you have found a system that works and you have all the cashflow that you need, plus the time to enjoy it, then it is a brilliant choice.

I suspect, if you are reading this book, it is because you want something more – you are searching for ideas on how to do something better.

Case study – make money from your property knowledge

In early 2011, we ran a series of three-day workshops to teach people 'How to Make More Money from Your Property Knowledge'. One of the delegates was a very detailed and data-driven type of personality. Her day job was filled with systems and organising things. It made perfect sense to her that her business would be around the systems and organisation of property investing. Helping others through resources she could easily design, develop and create.

It was totally congruent and in her flow. She organised herself and then reproduced this system into a replicable format. We are looking forward to the launch of her product and services.

Case study – retire as early as you want

I have been working with a client for the last six months, learning what she wants from life, her attitude towards risk and her financial situation. It all boiled down to a desire to retire early, to get away from the well-placed corporate job that was stopping her from having even more of the life she wanted. The biggest challenge was breaking through the traditional thinking that she had learned from parents, schools and other people she worked with. Gradually, I answered her questions and demonstrated that there was another way. I provided the evidence ROI. More importantly, she was able to check this out, independently, with her financial advisor. What more could you ask for than third party endorsement?

The client owned a relatively mortgage-free property and, like a lot of people, thought that retirement meant she had to pay off the mortgage to be free. What if I could get someone else to pay a bigger mortgage for her *and* give her money to live on?

I showed her the example I used in my first book, *Using Other People's Money: How to Invest in Property*. I demonstrated that by increasing her mortgage and leveraging that money through property investment she could own managed properties that produced enough cashflow to repay the property mortgages and the initial cost of borrowing from her home, and still have enough money to retire early! I am now in the process of building her retirement portfolio. Best of all, the financial advisor is watching from the side lines and considering his own investment portfolio. When she retires 7–10 years earlier than planned, her work colleagues will want to know how.

Chapter 5

Money – the reality

When you understand how the money market works and what lenders want, then all excuses to succeed fly out of the window. I will explain what various lenders want from their borrowers and how and where to get your information. There are risks and consequences and it is not all about having the 'right' state of mind, although that definitely helps!

Using credit cards to buy a property or fund a project

Like all lending, the most important thing before you start is to understand how much it is going to cost you to borrow the money, when you can pay it back and who is going to pay the interest in the meantime.

However, in its simplest form, a credit card if used properly can give you up to 45 days extra money – interest free. In its most strategic form, it can lend you most of the deposit or costs for an investment project at 0% interest for between 9 and 15 months! Your challenge, with everything associated to borrowing money, is to understand the money flow of your deal. When you will pay it back, where that money will come from, and who is going to pay the interest on the money while the project is being worked.

The next challenge is how to borrow money on a credit card without affecting your credit score. Please be aware that lenders share information behind the scenes as they are all owned by one massive shareholder – us, through the government. This means that even a last-minute application to a credit card, right before completion, could result in your mortgage offer being pulled – beware!

Money management system – stuff they really don't want you to know

Banks want you to stay ignorant of the game and how it works. On one hand, they want you to take out credit cards and buy stuff that really you can't afford, so that at the end of the month you can't clear your credit card balance and instead pay them an extortionate rate of interest. On the other hand, they now also want you to be a perfect borrower. From a secured lending perspective, the underwriters of mortgages need you to demonstrate that you know how to manage your money. The way that you can do this is to limit the amount of unsecured borrowing (credit cards) that you have available, clear your balances regularly, yet keep borrowing and paying back.

Now the experts out there will be telling you to apply for credit cards, because you need to show you can manage your money and also, if you have access to credit on cards, then you can buy their expensive courses. What you must understand is how a lender views the activity on your credit record and how this affects your credit score and, ultimately, your ability to borrow money through mortgages.

First, do not apply for too many credit cards at once or apply to have your existing cards increase their limits. Just by asking, you are affecting your credit score whether or not you are successful. Second, when you have cards, do not 'max them out' and use every last pound available to you, as you will look out of control and desperate for cash. Have a strategy to pay back your cards regularly and even overpay them now and then.

I am not going to go into any more detail about credit cards here as my first book, *Using Other People's Money*, covers this extensively. Suffice to say, credit cards are a brilliant tool if you know what to do. If not, then I have an e-book all about using credit cards. Again, please check the website at TheSourcersApprentice.com. Alternatively, read my first book.

What is gearing?

Gearing is a measure that a lender uses to measure how much you have actually borrowed, particularly on unsecured lending like credit cards, against how much available credit you have. You need to get to a position where you are borrowing under 50% of your potential borrowing, ie. have a gearing ratio of less than 50%. How do you work this out? Add up the total debt on all your credit cards and divide it by the total of all your credit limits.

I have guessed the figure of 50%. When I first increased my credit cards to cover my training costs, my credit rating dropped through the floor. I called the credit agencies and spoke with them – they can be very helpful. They explained about gearing and I started to experiment by paying off my 0% credit cards bit by bit as they came to the end of the life of the offers. I noticed that my credit rating started to improve as my gearing ratio moved towards 60%. Of course, other factors will have been at play – like the number of searches on my record, but I do believe gearing is now a significant decision-making factor.

Summary – good habits for managing your credit cards effectively

1. Get your credit reports and credit scores regularly – at least every other month – and check your information.
2. Minimise the number of applications you make to a maximum of one every other month and fewer than three in six months.
3. Don't reapply if you have just been turned down – wait until you get your credit reports, repair the problem and then wait again before continuing.
4. *Always* set up a direct debit payment and then overpay the minimum payment each month as you see fit.
5. Keep a spreadsheet and track each card, know your credit limit, know when you last asked for an increase, know when your 0% deal runs out and clear that card first.
6. Aim to bring your gearing ratio down by making focused payments.
7. Clear any cards that are accruing interest charges as a priority.
8. Remember, good debt is for purchases that earn you money (for example, a property purchase or refurbishment) and bad debt is the purchase of goods or services that reduce in value and cost you money.
9. Know how you will get the money back out of a deal to repay your cards and, if appropriate, who is paying the interest.

Playing the lenders at their own game

When I was in my poor phase as a single mother, literally counting every single 10 pence piece I spent, the credit card was my saviour. I put my university grant money in a high-rate deposit account and I made every purchase I could by credit card – while still knowing my budget and my income. I then cleared the credit card every month, in full, from the savings account – one withdrawal. At the end of the year, the bank gave me approximately £100 interest for managing my money, which the girls and I spent on our summer holidays and having fun.

It might not seem like a lot, but it was a great return (roughly 3–4% better than the building society) for relatively little effort, during a time when my budget for food and entertainment was very limited!

I later developed this skill and learned how to play the 0% off-set game. To work this strategy, you need an off-set or 'One' mortgage account. Then you borrow money at 0% from your credit card and deposit it into your off-set mortgage account. This effectively discounts your mortgage by the amount borrowed at 0% on your credit card. It's brilliant in today's market where it is better to off-set your mortgage as mortgage interest is 3–6% and savings interest only 1–2%. These accounts can then also become a personal source of pre-authorised lending and practically free borrowing.

Listen to the market experts

I knew nothing about this before I started to invest. I soon realised that if I wanted to borrow money in a challenging market, then I needed to understand what the people who were going to lend me money wanted from me. How did I find the information? By seeking out conversations with experts who know about the economy. Do you belong to the NLA (National Landlord Association)? They run lectures and, in Autumn 2011, had a representative from the Bank of England explain the thinking behind the interest rates. I wrote a report on the event – the reference is in the bibliography and at TheSourcersApprentice.com.

Listen to speakers at events – repeatedly ask people in the property industry what they think about the market and start to form an opinion. I keep getting newsletters saying that interest rates will go up – well, yes, of course they will, but not in the next month (at the time of writing this of course). How do I know this? If you check the Bank of England's monthly meeting reports where they discuss interest rates, you'll see that only one person wants rates to be increased! As that mood and number of votes change, then there is a real risk of immediate interest rates increasing. With inflation driven by energy prices rather than consumer spending, any increase in interest rates will not slow borrowing and inflation; it will kill any potential growth in high-street sales.

Risk and consequences

Having said this, you need to 'stress-test' all loans. What if interest rates go up by, let's say, 5%? What would your net monthly cashflow be? If less than £100, then maybe you need to rethink if the deal has enough cashflow to stand changes in the market – or maybe consider a 3–5-year fixed rate loan (subject to strategy of course).

Rates will go up. 'When?' is an educated question and subject to so many external factors that it is almost impossible to tell. Whatever happens, you need to be prepared! Know the risks and consequences of the debt you are taking on. That was how the off-plan and new-build buyers of years gone by failed. They thought they were buying a luxury flat for £3,000. Instead, they were trading £3,000 of actual cash for over £200,000 of liability – debt – a loan to be repaid!

Whatever strategy you decide and whatever amount of effort you put in to understand the money markets and economics, it is up to you. I would suggest that the more proactively responsible you are, the more you mitigate the risk of investing. The only one who can protect your family and your financial future and dreams is you! No blame, just responsibility, and with that comes more control and a refined decision-making ability.

A brief history – banking and the money markets

This section explains a little about commercial lending from my perspective and experience, and more about finance and lending in general.

During 2008 and 2009, the availability of money in the market place and high street was, as we know, severely constricted, as banks and mortgage lenders pulled out of the lending market, either through poor performance or simply the lack of trust and the resultant short supply of funds available to lend. They stayed out until mid–late 2011.

I needed to understand how 'money worked' so that in 2009, when I approached my high-street bank to see whether I could borrow money from them to invest in property, I could understand their business; what they needed from an ideal client. Moving to more commercial lending meant having conversations as a business client of the bank, which entails a whole different language.

I will explain what I understand about the money markets, how the banks work and then go on to explain how I have used commercial bank lending to invest in property.

I am not going to cover the whole history of banking, just a brief summary of key points that I think are important to set the scene from the banks' perspective. It is important to understand the origins of the money you eventually borrow from a bank.

In the old days (pre-1990), there were two sorts of banks; first consumer banks that collected savings deposits from, and lent to, ordinary people. These banks relied on and served people that worked and accumulated personal surplus cash, which they then deposited in the bank for safekeeping. This money was lent to other people for a fee. It was tangible real money and the bank only lent what it had. This system of banking was formulated in law through the Glass-Steagall Act, established in 1933–34 after the First World War, to prevent consumer banks from engaging in risky lending practices.

There were also investment banks, which were the accumulated wealth of a specific number of business partners who pooled their money and lent it to bigger projects and to businesses. They evaluated the risks carefully as they were lending their own money, however this was still considered a more speculative form of lending with higher risks and rewards. This was not something that should be done with consumer funds.

In the late 1990s during the Clinton administration, there was a move in America to merge the two types of bank. This had always been resisted as it had provided a safe feature, a form of compartmentalisation of lending risk. Ordinary people and their savings were handled in one way and slightly more speculative and higher risk lending was managed by people that could afford to gamble high risk for higher return.

1998 saw the merger of Citicorp and Travelers Group to create the largest financial services business in the world. This actually contravened the Glass-Steagall Act, however, instead of stopping the merger the business was given a 12-month reprieve in order that Alan Greenspan, Chairman of the Federal Reserve of of the United States (known as the Fed or Federal Reserve), and his colleagues could pass a new law allowing such mergers. This act, called the Gramm-Leach-Bliley Act, was passed on 12 November 1999 and became fondly known as the 'Citigroup Relief Act'!

This combined with later innovations in financial products (derivatives) caused the collapse in early 2000 and when we did not learn our lesson, it produced the world recession we are now in. By January 2001, just two years later, the American and world financial market was dominated by just five investment banks (Goldman Sachs, Morgan Stanley, Lehman Brothers, Merrill Lynch and Bear Stearns).

Financial innovation and the invention of derivatives flowed smoothly into the markets as the volume of lending exploded across the globe. Subprime mortgage lending in America quadrupled between 2000 and 2006. George W. Bush, to paraphrase, said something to the effect that no-one needs to live in a rubbish house just because they don't have the money to afford a decent one. So, instead of improving social housing people were encouraged to borrow vast sums of money to buy property in a booming market and we have all heard the phrase NINJA (no income, no job or assets) mortgages.

Derivatives, Collateralized Debt Obligations (CDO) and Credit Default Swaps (CDS) are topics that are so involved and fascinating that I might have to add that to my book list as well – called 'how the world sunk in a pile of paper debt, while the rich got richer'. That's not a knock at the bankers.

The people we refer to as 'the bankers' are really just employees of banks that were paid commission to sell products, the only difference is that the sale of a photocopier, utility supplier or holiday will not cause a country to go bankrupt (like Iceland, Greece and many others). These employees had a great job, maybe they had an obligation to question the real value of what they were selling and the risk to the investor?

The real 'bankers', those that earn hundreds of millions of pounds, are still all employed in senior political posts in the American government, ensuring that the status quo remains in their favour, and the favour of their friends! Anyone that spoke out about the financial system, or derivatives, or the need for regulation was disgraced, dismissed or discredited. The list is huge, but interesting reads are the papers and books produced by Raghuram Rajan, Eliot Spitzer, Satyajit Das and Charles Morris.

So why have I written so much about the American banking system? Because, what America does the world tends to follow. British banks also operated in the derivatives market, our lenders lent 125% mortgages, we had self-certified mortgages. Anyone could borrow, everyone did and the money was not always repaid!

There is still a small part of banking business built around lending money that a bank has received as deposits from savers. Most lending funds are now largely 'bought' and traded on the money markets. This has become a major industry in its own right across the world.

The money, in some senses, still comes from 'people' who have surplus cash, just on a massive and inconceivable scale. You may have heard the comment that trillions and trillions of pounds are circulating around the globe at any one time. The problem is that instead of always lending real tangible money or paper notes backed by gold deposits held in vaults, banks now lend 4, 10 or 40 times the actual money they have to back them up. In recent years, you may have noticed that your credit card limits or bank overdrafts have been reduced without warning. This is because lenders will have technically promised you, in advance, that you can use that money if you need it. Now, they need it; they want to lend it to other people for a fee, not have it sitting there 'just in case' you might want it!

What does the future hold? More of the same sadly! No matter what Europe proposes in terms of regulation, America with its powerfully placed advocates of high-risk (and high-reward – consequences be damned) lending will never agree. If Obama, with a mandate for change, has appointed all the leaders of the system that created the crisis to positions of power to change the system what do you think is going to happen?

We need to start the money moving at the bottom of the food chain again, we need to get spending personally and commercially, in a responsible and calculated way to promote business and commerce. We need to go round the outside of these major banks and investment houses to the private individuals with money. These people have also been failed by a system designed to support the 'uber-rich' on a scale that we cannot even comprehend. Know what you have to offer, know what is in the deal for a client or partner and then get talking to people.

Money costs – LIBOR sets the rate

The banks can 'buy' money for a fee. The average interest rate calculated on a daily basis is called the LIBOR rate (London Interbank Offered Rate). This is best explained as the interest rate that banks pay for the money they borrow. They can choose to borrow money for set periods and LIBOR has rates for three or six months, and one or more years. It is quite interesting to look at these rates and see how they change over time. Analysts use this information as a measure of the confidence in the market and to predict future interest rates.

So, if you want to borrow from Birmingham Midshires, their primary bank HBOS may have actually bought or borrowed the money they are lending to you on the open market. Let's say they are being charged 2.5% – they need to make a profit on that money. They have to cover their business costs.

Let's say that to lend you £100,000 it costs the bank 2.5%, *plus* they have to pay staff, systems, premises and marketing. Assume they need to charge about 9% to cover all these costs and make a profit. Now they can't charge 9% when the base rate at the bank of England is just 0.5%!

So, they charge a fee of 3% to cover 'administration costs':

£100,000 x 3% = £3,000

If you divide that evenly over 12 monthly mortgage payments, that is like paying another £250 a month – it's a good job you can add it to the loan!

So, if your real mortgage rate is 5.49% and you take out the borrowing on a one-year term, then in effect you are paying a rate of closer to 8.45% (as you add the 3% fee to the mortgage rate). If the tie-in period for the mortgage is two years, then you can apportion the admin fee over the two years so, in real terms, your mortgage rate would be 5.49 + 1.5 = 6.99%.

The bottom line is banks that have lost lots of money in the past, need to make a profit now. Some have a massive business debt to repay the taxpayer! This is why there is this tension between the Bank of England's low base rate and relatively high lending rates, coupled with (in my opinion) high lender fees.

When you take out a loan, consider the cost of the lender fees alongside your interest rate and the term of the tie-in period of the loan. Initially, you will probably want a one-year mortgage rate to enable you to remortgage the property and circulate your cash investment. When you are ready to remortgage, you will need to consider your strategy and attitude towards risks, as well as the overall performance of your portfolio before you can decide which new lending product is most appropriate for your needs.

I would suggest that you choose the longest term you can get, with the best rates of course, that meets your strategic needs. The long-term products will help you to spread the cost of the high lender fees over a longer period and effectively make the process of remortgaging cheaper. However, this does not necessarily mean that you have to have a fixed rate – that is a choice based on interest rates.

As a final point, LIBOR and banks buying money on the open market explains why you are charged early redemption penalties. The bank will have borrowed the money it is lending to you from someone else for a set period. If you give the money back, then the bank is no longer receiving interest payments from you, yet will still have to pay them or re-lend the money with associated increased admin costs. The bank needs you to borrow the money for the same or similar period that they have borrowed it for. That is why certain lending products come and go in the market. The bank will have been able to borrow at a specific rate and when that money is all lent out, they will have to borrow again at a new rate – so creating a new lending product.

Why go commercial?

The best reason to go commercial is because the bank will consider you as a complete person or business, unlike mortgage lenders who see you as a credit score and a specific property. They will also 'create' or offer you a lending product that is bespoke to the risk that you present. This means that the more successful they consider you and the lower risk you present, then the more preferential the terms of the loan.

Lending or a mortgage – what's the difference, what's the point?

The main difference is in the philosophy or culture of the organisations that are lending you the money, and that's very noticeable. The banks are old and in some senses old-fashioned institutions. They are a contradiction of highly-cautious and yet the most extraordinary risk takers in the history of humankind.

When you start a conversation with a bank about commercial lending, they will want to follow a very similar process to a mortgage lender, but you will need to present yourself very differently. They will want to know that you are a safe business for the money they are going to lend you. They will check your credit score but, more importantly, they will meet you face to face and want to understand your business model, how it works, where you make money and why it is a good idea. You will need to explain and justify your strategy – this means you need your research and facts to hand.

Commercial lenders will want details of your existing business and investments, details of your income, expenditure, assets and liabilities. They will also want to know what cash you are going to put into the business or the deal. They are going to credit score you and also investigate your business model and your experience. As you can imagine, this is much more in depth and initially time consuming than applying for a decision in principle (DIP), but for some of you it might be worth being considered as a whole entity. If this all sounds too daunting, speak to your broker and explain that you want to approach a commercial bank. They will be able to help and advise you. If not, do it yourself. You have nothing to lose and everything to gain.

If you pass the 'interview' stage, the bank will want to know that they can obtain security for the money they are going to lend you. They will take, in principal, anything of a similar value. This means it does not have to be the actual house you are buying; it could be another unencumbered property or cash savings. In most cases, they will use the property you are buying and carry out a survey on it.

The terms for the lending are now negotiable! Which means, within reason, the better you are as a business proposition and the less risk you present, the more preferential the rates you can agree.

There are several components to a commercial loan:

1. The exposure or loan to value. In simple terms, how much is the bank prepared to lend you against the collateral you are offering? At the moment, they are mostly offering a maximum of 65%. However, you might be able to find higher.
2. The cost of the money or the interest rate. Now, it is important to be careful here, because most commercial lending is on a capital and repayment basis, not interest only like with buy-to-let mortgages. They use phrases like 'pay rate'. A pay rate of, for example 3.5%, means 3.5% over the base rate (which is currently 0.5%) giving a total loan rate of 4% capital and repayment (this will feel like a rate of 7%+ if it is an interest-only equivalent loan).

3.   Coverage. This means that you must have sufficient income (rent) to cover the cost of repaying the debt. Banks express this as a percentage. In a normal buy-to-let mortgage, they look for 125% coverage. All commercial banks will be different but, essentially, they do not count the full annual rent as income, they assume a percentage of void and maintenance costs. So they may only consider 70% of rental income and then expect that to cover the loan cost by a rate of 160%, for example. You will need to really understand this part of your agreement; otherwise, you may find that none of your deals will actually be acceptable.

4.   Finally, there is the term of the loan. As with normal mortgages, this will be based on age. However, because the bank assumes that you will keep the loan and clear it in full through monthly payments (capital and repayment), then this can make your monthly payments quite high and in turn affect your ability to provide rental cover. They will refer to the amortization of the loan, how the capital portion of your mortgage reduces the actual debt.

Commercial lending is really easy to understand once you put yourself in the position of the lender. They want to lend money safely, knowing that you can afford to repay the debt and, if not, that they have sufficient security to recoup their money if need be.

Why is commercial lending a good idea?

There are three great reasons:

1.   Much cheaper fees. Unlike mortgage companies, banks do not charge 2–3.5% admin fees; fees can be just a few hundred pounds. However, the surveys can cost about £500 instead of £300.

2.   Banks do not operate a 'six-month rule' on commercial lending. So they do not mind if the vendor only bought the property three months ago.

3.   They do not charge 'early redemption charges'. Therefore, although there is a term (length) to the loan, you are not tied into that lending product like with buy-to-let mortgages.

Now consider points 2 and 3 together. This means that you could buy any property you like (providing it meets the lending criteria) and then either resell it on the open market or remortgage it after refurbishment at closer to its full market value at the six month stage, rather than waiting a year for the buy-to-let term to end.

Different is good

This is a different way of borrowing money and, like with credit cards, you need to understand what the lender wants to achieve and what they want from you.

1. Are you the owner of a sound business, well justified with appropriate experience?
2. Can you provide appropriate levels of collateral, either through other investment properties or assets of value?
3. Can you afford to pay back the loan? Can you prove that you can cover the cost of the debt through the rent on the property and through a partner's employed income?
4. Ultimately, the lender wants to know whether or not you are going to be a good customer from whom they can make money.

Certainly, in my case, they really liked the fact that Bob, my partner, was employed and had a regular income – this provided additional security and peace of mind. The bank obviously wanted us to transfer our business account to them – that was no problem. They were happy that we (temporarily) deposited a fair-sized cash lump sum in the account, which we later drew out over a couple of months and paid back to our off-set mortgage. The need to have a salary in the business partnership is definitely becoming a requirement with most lenders.

Think like a professional investor, present yourself as a serious and knowledgeable business owner, show the bank you know what you are talking about and have a track record of success, or that you are planning to have a track record of success.

So what do lenders like HBOS and The Mortgage Works want?

The reason I started with commercial lending is because 'off-the-shelf' mortgage lenders like Birmingham Midshires (HBOS) and The Mortgage Works want the same things as commercial lenders. They want to know that you will pay them back and that they can make a profit.

The difference is that with HBOS or The Mortgage Works you are one of hundreds and hundreds of mortgage applications a day going through a massive centralised system. You are on a conveyor belt and they can pick and choose the best applications based on whether or not they have lent out all of the money that they planned to.

Rather than see you as an individual business with a business plan and strategy to back it, you are simply a way for them to hit their lending targets. Yes, you will get an interest-only mortgage, but this comes as a non-negotiable product (off the shelf) with tie-in periods and hefty admin costs. Both commercial and off-the-shelf lenders have a role to play – it all depends on your strategy.

Chapter 6

The rules – facts and figures

I will limit this chapter to just a series of headlines and pointers, as the detail is so volatile and changeable that you will need to check *everything* with your broker.

As it stands at the moment there are a series of rules, conditions and considerations that you need to take into account when costing the finance for any specific deal. To some of you, this chapter will not be news. But for many of you, this will be very valuable and possibly save you from a dreadful deal.

I was recently talking to some investors who I considered quite experienced. In the process of the conversation, they explained a specific deal, which was a redevelopment they planned to sell on within two months of purchase – this was when I realised that there are still investors not aware of all of the ins and outs of financing a deal.

The six-month rule

During 2008, lenders started to clamp down on the process of buying a property at discount and then immediately remortgaging it at market value. The famous and classic system was with Mortgage Express. It was initially used on new-build developments, but soon started to spread to existing houses as the market moved away from off-plan and new build.

All no money down (NMD) strategies are designed to get around the fact that lenders only want to lend you a percentage of the purchase price.

The actual rule was recommended by the Council of Mortgage Lenders and adopted over time by lenders. The rule means that a lender will not lend money for the purchase of a property where the vendor has not already owned it for six months.

The crucial date for most lenders is the date of completion and this is required to be recorded on the Land Registry. Now this is an optionally adopted rule and in Chapter 5 on page 91 I pointed out that most commercial lenders are not bothered by this, whereas nearly all high-street, off-the-shelf lenders do apply the rule. You must be aware that this rule applies to investor *or* residential buyers, especially using the HBOS group and the other buy-to-let lenders.

Early redemption charges or penalties (ERC/ERP)

Most off-the-shelf lenders will want to know that they have lent you money for a specific time. This is nothing to do with the term of the mortgage, usually between 15 and 25 years. This is to do with the commitments they have made to borrow that money from the money markets.

An ERC or ERP varies from lender to lender and, for example, might be 3% of the loan if the loan is redeemed in the first year of the product term, reducing to 1% in the third year of a product term.

You must check the tie-in periods of any mortgage product that you are considering; otherwise the projected profit or cash released on remortgage can be significantly less.

Again, there are a number of lenders who do not charge ERC, these are mostly building societies. With the benefit of no ERC comes the 'penalty' of a higher interest rate or a lower loan to value. This is something to consider carefully in your calculations.

Putting ERC with the six-month rule

So, if your intention is to buy, refurbish and sell a property in under a year, the following conditions would need to apply:

1. To locate a mortgage product without a tie-in period and therefore no ERC.
2. To understand that any remortgage or sale of the property would need to be funded by a lender who did not operate under the six-month rule.
3. Or wait six months before you complete on the sale.

This means that the majority of people who are looking to buy and get 'all their money back out in six months' have not really considered all the constraints on that strategy. The hardest hit are builder-developers, who turn a derelict property back into decent home standards!

Remortgaging takes 12 months not six

This follows the same principle. The first purchase loan must be either a one-year product or a product without penalties. Then you have to consider the second 'remortgage' lender, as they will still be able to apply the six-month rule.

It is possible to use a combination of commercial first mortgage and then remortgage to an off-the-shelf lender. It might also be possible with some lenders as long as the owners remain identical. When I tried to remortgage a property bought under our joint venture commercial funding and then remortgage it using just one name (as that is better for tax purposes), I had a terrible job explaining that this did not constitute a sale! Beware.

If you are looking to release significant equity to get your investment cash back out into circulation, you will also need to consider the surveyor companies that lenders use. Each surveyor will have a patch and they will know the properties and their histories. Without significant upward movement in the market, you will be unlikely to release £30,000 for just a coat of paint. The surveyors have long memories and will want to see capital improvements.

The cost of bridging

I have yet to find a deal, personally, where the profit is still significant enough to take the risk of buying using bridging finance. Remember that the combination of the six-month rule and lender awkwardness means that you must budget and plan for at least nine months (in my opinion), otherwise the penalties could be crippling.

Work carefully with your broker to make sure that all of the numbers stack up and that your profit projections have included sufficient contingencies, then double-check these figures with the brokerage house. Make sure that you have worked through and understood all of the costs.

Cash out – I base my figures on 2 for 1

I mentioned in the Introduction on page 6 that someone contacted me and asked for a copy of all my deals over the last year, as they had not been able to find a deal where they could get all of their money back out in six months (hence writing this section). Even without the additional constraints applied by mortgage lenders, this strategy requires a stable or rising market to guarantee success. I am not sure exactly what is happening as you are reading this book, but I bet that the market is still volatile! This strategy not only relies on prices holding, but also requires a surveyor to agree with your calculations one year in the future. I can't rely on a surveyor to confirm a price on a month-by-month basis.

When I demonstrate my projections to clients, not only am I extremely cautious, but I also estimate *no* increase in property value (as caused by normal inflation, which is running at approximately 5%), no change in loan to values calculations and just the average street value less £5,000 (contingency).

I would rather a client, or myself, came to remortgage a property and was delighted that they had managed to pull most of their money back out, rather than risk disappointment.

I have a demonstration that shows clients the potential income and ROI from an investment pot of £200,000. It assumes that the money pulled out at the one-year remortgage is only half of the total buying costs. Remember, I assume buying costs to include solicitor fees, surveys, my fees, right through to refurbishment budgets, gas certificates and tenant find fees. I feel this is a more realistic set of figures to use. If the deal works on this basis, then it's a good deal.

Below market valuations (BMV) and surveyors

This has really been covered earlier, but I can't miss an opportunity for a moan about this strategy and the surveyors. I mentioned that surveyors can't be relied upon to agree with your figures. In fact, if you challenge a surveyor and they give in and agree with your valuation, then that impacts on their insurance.

Valuations are so subjective, yet really they shouldn't be. I have just had two surveys by the same lender and same valuation company on the same property. The result… one surveyor wanted a retention to repair the chimney leading and the gutter (£2,500 for just £250 of work!), the other never mentioned the roof and wanted an electrical report!?

At one point, I had four purchase surveys and two remortgages taking place all on the same day with the same lender. The properties were in four different areas of the city; they included three houses and three flats. There were three surveyors and the one carrying out the remortgages was greeted at the property and offered a pack of local comparables. Every single property (all six, in four different areas, with three different surveyors and two property types) came back exactly £5,000 less than the requested valuation figure. How is that possible?

Ultimately, like the banks, surveyors got carried away with themselves and the rising property market in the mid 2004–2007. They overvalued the assets and under-considered the rental implications of large blocks of city-centre flats. This is effectively a double backlash; first against past overvaluations and second against the actual availability of funds. You just have to live with it. No doubt you saw details of the court case in 2011, where the court ruled that 'a surveyor was employed by the lender to carry out the valuations on their behalf and *did not* owe the purchaser a duty of care'. Okay, so that is surveyors well and truly dismissed and disgraced!

To finish the topic of valuations and surveys the 'bulls**t valuations' that were bandied about in 2010 and 2011 need explaining. Have you come across the deal packagers that offer you a property at 30% BMV and all your money back out in...? Or worse, they packaged the financials too and made the deal NMD? I won't labour my opinion about the legalities, other than to say there was a significant increase in the number of reported fraudulent attempts to gain mortgages and discovered fraudulent mortgage applications from mid 2011 onwards. Worse than fraud, this strategy reduced the so-called investors' cashflow and created a portfolio of highly-geared properties.

Lease options – the rules still apply

This is still a relatively new and untested strategy in the UK. The early structures sent investors down a lease pathway that meant they could not complete on the deal in three, five or seven years time, because of the six-month rule and the deal structure needed to resell to a tenant buyer on an assignable contract. If you don't understand what I have just said and you are currently pursuing a lease option strategy, you might need to get advice and check how you are structuring your deals.

I have also mentioned lease options under the return on time section in Chapter 3, page 49, where I commented that this strategy (and you could argue any strategy) takes a lot of time to get right. I think a lease option strategy takes longer to get right because you are effectively speaking to desperate and distressed people at a time of high emotion about a new form of finance that is not widely understood in the UK.

I would really urge you to consider all the same buying rules for a property as you would if you were going to proceed with a purchase and a mortgage. By taking on these leases, you are taking on the commitment of the property. You need to be clear that the monthly return will give you significant income in return for your time.

I know some lease option trainers talk about 'tenant buyers' taking on all the responsibility, but as with the words 'passive income', there is no such thing as something for nothing. This tenant buyer still needs monitoring; after all they are actually your asset – not the property because you don't own that! The money is in the hands of the tenant buyer!

So why do you need buying rules for lease options? Because at the end of the lease term you still need to make this deal work as either a purchase or sale. If you are going to buy it yourself, will the property cashflow as a rental under the new increased mortgage? The mortgage will increase because the rates will change. If you are planning to sell, who is your target vendor and can they afford to finance the purchase? Not every deal has a tenant buyer in the mix. In the meantime, you still need to cover the cost of the current owner's mortgage, insurance and possibly repair costs and void periods while making a profit. How much do you need or want in exchange for your time and possibly your stress?

Remember the basics...

These are just some of the headline facts and figures, rules and conditions you need to consider on any deal that you are thinking of buying. Run the numbers – overestimate costs and underestimate profits – if the deal still works, great, it sounds a beautiful one. If the numbers are border line, recheck and reconsider. I remember a quote from Richard Branson, 'Businesses are like buses – there is always another one coming along...'. I think properties are like buses; there is always another one coming along. It is better to miss one and get a comfortable seat than to spend the next 2–3 years chasing it down the street as it leaves with all your money.

Summary

I was very conscious when I came to the end of this section that it was much briefer than Section 1. Does this make it less important? Definitely not! It means that the economic environment is much more volatile and that is the one big disadvantage of writing a book – the time delay in publishing. Once written, life moves on and the words remain static.

I hope you recognise as you read this section that you will have to double-check everything for current relevance. My aim in mentioning all of the issues that are current now (some that may have already passed their time and some that may be still to come) is that you will have a broad base of understanding from which to conduct your own research.

So now we are at a point where you understand 'why' you want to invest. You have a critical understanding about money – how it flows, how it can be leveraged and how it can be measured to ensure return on that investment is the best possible use of your valuable resource. You also have the language of the lenders, whether they are banks or private individuals, and can demonstrate and explain why your investment opportunity is one not to be missed.

Now it's time to move on to the practical section – Section 3. Whether you are brand new to investing or have been buying for some time, Section 3 will take you through the process that I use to source properties step by step. Remember, I am my number one client, then my family's, joint venture partner's and my bespoke clients'. That does not mean that my bespoke clients get second-best deals or that I keep all the best deals for myself. Whoever has the money to invest is the person I shop for.

I buy properties to order. I do not randomly get deals and then try to place them. This means each person, myself included, gets the best possible deal available at that time. My time is very focused and each minute spent sourcing is paid for by a client or myself. I use my time wisely and find deals that use the investment cash wisely.

Section 3

Becoming a property business owner

Chapter 7

Getting practical

This section of the book contains the essence of how to set up and run a property sourcing business, by thinking and acting as the owner of a property sourcing business. The model and purpose of this book is designed to:

- Streamline your time, making it more effective and financially rewarding;

- Sharpen your focus on the best possible cashflowing deals; and

- Leverage all available resources – yours and other people's.

It is a simple model... based, of course, on a sound understanding of all the principles that have been described in the first two sections.

Just in case you have skipped forward to this section, I highly recommend that you take onboard the business concepts in Section 1 and the financial language and understanding of Section 2. Otherwise, I believe that your path to financial freedom will have a lot more bumps than necessary!

This section is now going to move through all the stages of finding and selling a property deal covering:

Getting started:

- Setting a budget;

- Choosing the right strategy, yield and cashflow;

- Understanding how the figures work; and

- Finding the right area.

Defining the area to property type and tenant type:

- Visiting the area;

- Viewing a house or two;

- Understanding estate agents;

- Drafting your list of property buying rules; and

- Understanding letting agents.

Running the numbers:

- Working out the true value of a property;

- Tips from a surveyor;

- Making an offer; and

- Return on investment (ROI) examples.

Building relationships:

- Understanding your personality type.

Understanding the service you are offering:

- Deciding what service to offer;

- Deciding what to charge;

- Finding investor clients; and

- Establishing the relationship.

The contract and paperwork:

- How you get paid – what you get paid for;

- Securing the deal;

- What to do if it all goes wrong; and

- What not to do.

Doing it all again, moving to the next level:

- Outsourcing;
- A brief word about systems; and
- Reputation and marketing.

Ready?

Setting the marketing budget and creating a business plan

Before you even start your business of investing it is going to cost you money, so you need to create a business plan – an income and expenses chart. Put in the amount you want to earn monthly (net) and then a budget for expenses. It does not matter how much you need to earn a month net, the figure is a tool to calculate how many deals you need to source and sell on. So if you wanted to earn £2,500 net per month and had expenses of £500 per month, then you need to source *at least* one property per month at £3,000.

I would suggest that you set a minimum marketing and research budget of £2,500–£5,000 per annum and plenty of time. You need to be sure that you can 'afford' to start this business financially and in terms of your commitments. Knowing these numbers helps to give you focus on what you need to earn; your business plan will help you to be focused on budgets, income and expenses. It did take me a while to understand how it was possible to create a business plan when I did not know the sales price of a property, but that's because I was focusing on the wrong thing. Your business plan simply states how much income you must generate to cover expenses and still leave you with a net profit – so, in effect, how many deals you need to source or properties giving you cashflow you need to own.

In your marketing budget you will need to allow money for travel and accommodation, depending on where your areas for research turn out to be. You will need money to buy food while you are there if you are staying over.

Depending on your phone tariff, you will increase your call costs. You might increase printing costs as you gather your research into a file.

How much time can you spare? Are you working full time? When will you fit in your research? Are you prepared to use your annual leave to visit your chosen area for research and then later to buy deals? How much time can you take off work? I think the biggest thing that people miscalculate is the cost of personal time. Not just in this initial phase while you are all excited, but ongoing over the next two years while you build your connections, not only with contacts in your chosen area but also with those who will invest – your future clients.

If you can't commit for the first year to the following, then maybe you need to consider how seriously you want this new business:

- At least one evening a week networking. Pick one or two regular events that you can go to each month and then travel to other events to meet new people and see different areas. Budget for this is £960 over the first six months (four meetings at an average cost of £20 – which you may be able to reduce by pre-booking), plus a small budget for pre-meeting and post-meeting socialising in the bar (this is vital as it is where a lot of business happens, but you can drink a soft drink!) and travel costs.

- Saturdays – to research your area, track property prices, spot new properties for sale and analyse deals.

- Then, I would say, once every three weeks minimum take a trip to your area for a day. Ideally, do this during the week, but not Mondays as many estate agents have sales meetings first thing. Find the days your agents offer viewings and visit then. This trip can easily scale back to once a month, once you have a relationship with the estate agents but it should be supported with calls and emails between visits.

- Each visit would have a budget of £50 per night for accommodation (maybe less depending on where you are in the country), £50–£100 round trip petrol or transport costs, then a budget to eat while away from home, as two-day-old homemade sandwiches are nasty. Say, two nights

– giving two full days on location for the first six months. Fifteen visits at about £250 each is £3,750.

Okay, let's move on to the area – you can always refine the budget later once you have chosen your target area and worked out the costs more precisely.

More assumptions

The whole of this third section will assume that you are starting a sourcing business and then going to use your success to build it to a point where in 2–3 years (once you have appropriate accounts – and that is really important) you can give up work – safe in the knowledge that you will still be able to acquire mortgages.

If you have a secure relationship with a life or business partner, you may be able to move this date forward and rely on them as the core mortgage host for your own personal portfolio. By mid 2011 lenders were already requiring property investors to cover rental income with a supplementary PAYE salary in excess of £20,000–£25,000. And the European Parliament was threatening regulation to rule out rental cashflow in affordability calculations.

Sadly, lenders may not consider rental income as part of your accounts, so you will need to source deals or have some other property-related business. To earn £30,000 profit, you will need to source approximately 15–20 deals at £5,000 each subject to expenses and costs. This profit either covers your home costs or is providing the start of your personal investment pot. I also assume that you are planning to develop and refine your sourcing business and then take it to the next level. It is vital that you do not make decisions about 'early retirement' without securing your future mortgage-ability first and that will take accounts with profit!

Choosing the right strategy – I know why, now how do I start?

So how do you get started? I will assume that you are going to start with a relatively easy 'cashflow' model of investing – finding properties with a great ROI for investors looking to benefit from better cashflow for their money.

The reason I am starting with this strategy is that cashflow is everything. We are at a time of unprecedented low interest rates so this is the best time to benefit from high cashflow and, if you can't get it from a deal now, then is it really a great deal? Also, with a slow sales market and flat lining house prices, any refurbishment and quick flipping strategies for capital gain is a challenge, even before the lenders apply their rules and conditions.

Then there is the tax advantage – to buy, wait for appreciation and remortgage is effectively tax-free money to shop again. To buy and sell, is a taxable gain, which means that when you reinvest your cash in the second property it is 20–40% less than the profit you made on the first house! And I have to end with my opinion that buying to sell is a high-risk strategy – I want 'guaranteed' returns.

Yield and cashflow

If we are looking for high cashflow, then the first financial tool that I would use to define where in England I would buy is yield. Yield takes the gross rent per annum and divides it by the sale price on a property-by-property basis (you can average this for an area). Personally, I would look for areas where the yield is at least 10%. What you will be able to see if you are moderately good at maths is a pattern emerging. Rent needs to be high in proportion to a low-ish purchase price. Let me show you some examples:

Monthly rent	Annual gross rent	House price	Yield
500.00	6,000.00	100,000.00	0.06
500.00	6,000.00	75,000.00	0.08
550.00	6,600.00	65,000.00	0.10
600.00	7,200.00	100,000.00	0.07
600.00	7,200.00	75,000.00	0.10
700.00	8,400.00	75,000.00	0.11
700.00	8,400.00	200,000.00	0.04

You can already start to see a pattern. Where can you find rents on a buy-to-let property that are between £550 and £700 (or more) per month, but equally house prices that are low at £65,000 to £75,000? (Remember that this is the 'asking price' if you are working this out using Rightmove.) You can start to refine areas and assume a moderate discount on purchase price afterwards. Starting this way finds an area and buying a property under the asking price means that you will be able to find an even better corner of your area.

How do the figures work?

I spoke about yield as being the first 'financial tool' you can use to find an area, but by simply using Rightmove you can locate areas that meet your buying requirements. In fact, I no longer use yield as a measure after making that first decision. I personally find that yield lacks the level of true cost detail that I want when making a decision to buy a specific property.

For example, two properties both costing £60,000 and both giving a rental figure of £500 per calendar month would give the same yield:

£500 x 12 = £6,000 (annual rent)

£60,000 (purchase price)

= 10% yield

What yield does not factor in is the cost of refurbishment, if required, to achieve the market rent of £500. One property might have double glazing, gas central heating, a good kitchen and bathroom. It might only need a little decoration and some carpet costing, say, £1,500.

The other property might need double glazing, a new kitchen and full redecoration costing, say, £7,000. That would bring comparative costs to £61,500 verses £67,000. That's why I use ROI as my ultimate financial weapon. This figure explains, on a buy and hold strategy, exactly how much the money you have invested has earned you in rental payments (the equivalent of interest if the money stayed in the bank). It will also factor in any differences caused by loan to values and interest rates, because it considers the actual money earned and compares that to the actual total money spent.

The formula for ROI is:

Net annual rent = rent − (mortgage, letting agent fee and insurance cost)

Total cash invested = deposit + (solicitor's fees, survey, broker fee, refurbishment costs and tenanting costs)

Using this formula, I can compare a wider range of properties in one broad geographic area until I find the specific property types, number of rooms, level of refurbishment, even the streets I want to invest in.

What lies behind this formula is an understanding of the cost of money, and how leveraging money enables an investor to borrow from a wider range of sources while benefiting from the ongoing monthly cashflow. This is so important that I will come back to the numbers again in detail later, as the more times you read this the easier it will be to understand.

Start with Rightmove and find the right area

Start with Rightmove – you can either be systematic and write geographic locations down on a list and work through them, or you can start with places where you have been (that's how I started) or places nearest to you and then work outwards.

Enter the location address in Rightmove, this can just be the name of a town or area and select 'houses' and 'three bedrooms' as your filters to start – mainly because there is not a lot of difference in some places between two and three bedrooms when you compare it to rental income, size of property and potential future developments and strategy options. Literally do the same (I find it easier to use a second window) with rental properties (like for like).

Start looking for areas where a relatively low asking price is found in the same location as a reasonable rental value. Depending on how you start this strategy – the town you pick and where you live – you could find an area in two hours or two days. Think about it logically – think about how far you are prepared to travel.

I started by saying that you should find an area where the yield is 10%, just because you need to start somewhere. If you find an area relatively near to home that has a 9% yield, then that is great! As the slightly lower figure is off-set by time–cost savings and ease of working!

Once you have found a few areas (I would suggest maybe two or three) start to research the area itself. What is employment like? What are the council plans for area development, housing and businesses? There are loads of websites that you can use, including Mouseprice, local council sites, even local business sites and then, of course, the old-fashioned method of speaking to a human! Don't wait to find three areas before you get started – take action on this – put in the time. Don't fall into the 'anal-ising' trap.

What type of property are you looking for?

This does depend on your strategy of course. For example, if you wanted to rent a HMO (house of multiple occupation) to students, then finding out the development and business plan of the university would be critical. The same principle applies to any investment, whether it is buy-to-let, commercial, a flat or a house. Who is your tenant type and what affects them? What can increase their 'value' as an asset? What could have a detrimental effect?

If you are going to target employed, maybe even professional, tenants, then you will need properties close to transport links or close to employment. You might also need parking if they are going to commute by car. Next, you would need to understand the industry and business they are in (for example, city workers, factory workers and hospital workers), so research the employer and other employers in the area. What are their plans? I would also consider the consequences of that employer closing down, moving or downsizing. What other work opportunities are there? Find out if local employers run a scheme to relocate their employees. Could you advertise on their notice board or intranet?

If your preferred tenant type is unemployed, then what is the council's system for housing people on the social housing list? How many are waiting to be housed? How does the council operate its benefit system? How does it set the local housing benefit rates? You will start to develop a picture of the local area, its employment opportunities and stability, the council and how it operates and the local housing benefit system (what it pays and how it works).

For example, in London you can (in some local council areas) become a landlord who supplies property to the council on a longer lease basis, for example for 1–5 years. These schemes are very demanding, time limited and prone to cancellation at short notice so beware. The phrase used to describe this is 'Social Housing Landlord Schemes' or 'rent guaranteed schemes'. Once you have a relationship with the council, it can be easier to build up your reputation and the personal contacts necessary to provide a level of security for your properties and lease contracts.

This is the system that operates most of our London portfolio. Having said this, one property was cancelled with 24-hours notice and there was nothing I could do. If they don't need your property, they will just give it back!

In the north of England, a lot of councils have decided to work with local housing associations, contracting out the responsibility to house people on the social housing list. Many of these agencies will renovate or build and own their own stock, and so do not look to private landlords as a source of property.

In West London, there are a number of available schemes, from working with a specific local estate agent who manages the process, to some in-house council schemes that provide incentives to take higher risk tenants. Think about your strategy – your clients – the management of any problems – how quickly can you fill a vacant property? What ongoing skills and time commitment will your client need to manage this type of property?

Narrowing down the areas – time for a visit?

As you work through your area research, you will naturally develop your strategy and refine your area. Don't get distracted and keep coming back to why you are doing this – cashflow! I got repeatedly distracted as I learnt about new strategies – HMOs, lease options, etc. Remember what you are looking for. All these other strategies are tools that you can apply *if* your main strategy does not work on a particular property. I very rarely bother and once you find what works, just do it again and again. Why waste time?

Depending on how much time you put into your research strategy, you could be ready to visit an area within a week. Once you see a place in real life it may send you right back to your desk research. The great thing now is that you can visit an area virtually through Google Street View, so take a virtual tour first to avoid any shocks or wasted trips.

Google Street View, again, is a small step in narrowing down your wider choice of areas – remember to take a look down side roads and around the back of properties if you can. Check out the employment areas, the shops, the schools and the various residential areas. You will be surprised where the camera cars have been. Remember, broadly speaking, each 'town' will have an area preferred by students, the affluent, families, professionals and unemployed – see if you can mark these out on a map.

Recognise that, depending on where you currently live, some parts of London and England are very deprived, run down and have high levels of unemployment. I believe that we can regenerate an area one house at a time providing decent housing for families and children and decent investments for astute investors. Councils certainly don't have the budgets! Having said this, you don't need to start investing right in the middle of a war zone. Choose the edge of a planned regeneration area, understand the council's plans and realise the effects of the austerity measures on these plans and their timescales.

Now for the real visit

If you still like the sound (and sight) of an area, then it is time for a visit. This visit will have two purposes: one to check local research and 'get a feel for the place'; and two to make contacts. I would suggest booking into a local, cheap hotel and staying over at least one night as you want to be able to have a drive around after dark. You want to check out morning traffic flows and see your area in all its glory at different times of the day.

By staying over you will also have more flexibility in making appointments to see people. I would suggest that most estate agents or letting agents will be happy to see you when you walk through the door. However, you may need to book an appointment to speak to the local councils.

Plan this visit carefully – think about what you want to find out, confirm or rule out. All the time, keep your tenant type in mind. Much of this is personal choice or, dare I say, prejudice. I initially set out to house professional tenants, so I wanted property on easy transport links to local areas of employment or relatively near local employers.

I assumed that people travelled to work by train, like in London. In fact, local buses were the transport of choice and this widened the search area for investment opportunities. I then started to speak to local agents and viewed properties in keeping with this strategy – the numbers did not stack up. Vendors wanted too much money; they knew the perceived value of their assets in terms of yield and were not necessarily desperate to sell at a discount.

As my area knowledge increased, I discovered that the local housing system operated on a points system, which meant that the average unemployed person had to wait ages for a property. They still had growing families and needed homes. The local housing allowance (LHA) actually paid more, in certain areas, than the private rental rates, because the benefits office used an 'averaging system' to calculate the rates. So once I found a property in an area where LHA rates were higher than local rents, I had a potential benefit tenant catchment area.

I will add a word of caution here: I only decided to pursue this strategy because I developed a relationship with a local expert who knew the system and the local tenants extremely well. This is a more risky tenant type, but can also be a very profitable one.

It is all part of the visit planning – why are you going? What do you need to know to decide if this area is the right area to invest in? This does not have to be hard academic fact – provable in a court of law – this is still early research.

When should you view a property?

This is a tricky question. I wanted to see the properties straight away – I was in a new area and in order for me to get a real 'feel' for it I wanted to see the inside of properties for sale and get a sense of what a local agent meant by 'in need of modernisation'. I love that phrase. Four words that can mean anything from 'needs redecorating' in West London to 'this property has no central heating, a new species of mould on the back wall and a tree growing out of the bedroom window' the further outside of London you get!

This, again, refers back to your budget – how much time and cash have you allocated to developing your business and researching your market?

Understanding estate agents

This is as important as understanding the lending market. I am assuming again that you don't have money to burn and that you are not an internet whizz-kid. Along with that, I am also assuming that you are not going to start placing newspaper adverts or developing lead generation websites from day one. Even if you do have these skills and/or lots of money, I would counsel against it until you are sure that your strategy will work in the area you have chosen.

So your first port of call is an estate agent. Their sole (and soul) purpose is to sell you a property. They want to work with professional people who know what they are talking about and keep their word. That should not sound daunting because you are professional – you are setting up your own property investment business. You do know what you are talking about and, more importantly, asking questions about because you have carried out your research and you have a specific reason for your visit – questions you want answered. You will, of course, keep your word – that goes without saying.

Now some estate agents (especially small local offices) will take time to talk to you about the area – offer you a cup of tea and see you as someone whom they want a relationship with. Others are hardnosed commission-making money machines. If they don't recognise you as having cash in your pocket (burning a hole right now), then you will get a degree of 'don't waste my time' attitude.

Remember, they are employees; in most cases, they neither own investment properties nor are looking to. They have been trained by the school system and society to be sales machines and value money as a real thing – rather than understanding leverage like you do. They will dress flash, have pointed shoes, trendy haircuts and, if they drive a car, it will be fashionable too! You know about assets and liabilities, you know about ROI – you will be financially free and enjoying life long before they make manager!

They are employees and you are a business owner. You are there to interview them to see who you will pick to become your 'business partner', because as your business grows so will their commission! It's a variation on imagining them naked. I have interviewed my bank manager, my estate agents and my letting agents. I never told them obviously.

What does the estate agent need out of the conversation?

What does the estate agent want? The answer is easy – to know that you will help them to achieve their targets either for viewings or for sales.

What can you do to help?

See a few properties – maybe even make an offer or two. But *caution,* know that you can follow through if you get accepted. Personally, I would view half a dozen with each agent to find out the answers to the following questions (but I would not make any offers unless I had the cash to invest):

1. What are typical three-bedroom properties like in the area?
2. What are two-bedroom properties like?
3. What do the words in the description mean in reality?
4. What is the local construction like – is it Victorian terrace, or 1960s council?
5. Are gardens important?
6. Are most bathrooms upstairs or down?
7. What is the state of most kitchens and bathrooms in this price range?
8. What is the standard of décor?
9. Do local people prefer carpet or laminate, curtains or blinds, paint or paper?

Now, to get a balanced understanding of the local area you will need to view 'distressed' and possibly repossessed properties, mid-range family homes and maybe even something that is already under offer (find out the agreed price if you can). Be upfront, saying you are new to the area and want to find where your strategy will fit. Tell the estate agents what you are thinking of buying and who you want to rent to. Ask them the best areas.

I would repeat this process with at least four agents on your first visit. That's why you need to stay for two days!

By the time you return home, you will have an amazing understanding of an area – how and whether it fits your strategy, which agents you could maybe work with and which are idiots. I even received two email complaint letters when I placed under market value offers in an area where the estate agents felt they could sell for asking price – so what? I don't have to go to that estate agent again. I have to admit that at the time I was embarrassed, shocked and a thousand other feelings. BUT then I remembered that they were in a job and I was building a business and I need never see them again as they were just one of 10 agents in one area. So much of this business will be based on personality – you will love one agent and another person will loathe them – that's fine. Build *your* relationship based on *your* strategy for *your* business.

Time to review your research

I recommend that after your first visit you come back home and reflect on what you now know. You should have a starting area. You might change this in the future, but I would suggest that if it meets the following criteria, start the process of working out your investment model:

- Does the yield offer 9–10%?
- Do the cheaper properties sit in relatively decent areas where your tenant (not you) would feel at home?
- Have you found 2–4 agents who you could build a relationship with?
- Do you understand the local geography, employment and council area?

If you don't have enough information to decide on a local tenant type and appropriate property type, then you will either need to do more research or visit your second choice area.

When you do have enough information, you will need to refine the research further and create your buying rules. The rules make it easier for the estate agents and letting agents to understand exactly what you are looking for – it is, in a sense, your shopping list.

Your property buying rules

The rules bring everything together so far. At the beginning of this process, you needed to understand *why* you were planning to invest in property – what you wanted the result of property investment to be and your life to be like. Then you looked at the realities of your personal financial position. You have worked out the cashflow you want the business to produce, the level of involvement you want to have and your exit strategy. Now you need to draft out your list of 'property buying rules'.

My rules address the following issues:

- Purchase price – I personally want to buy below stamp duty threshold and I have defined this further as my area research helped me to create my investment model.

- Property type – I prefer houses as they often allow the opportunity for future development; you can't put a loft extension in a flat. Plus, I don't want to have a portfolio heavy with maintenance and service charges that I can't control, which is the downside of buying flats.

- Area – this is determined initially by yield and then strategy; it can be defined further by property type and tenant type.

- Number of rooms – I have calculated that a three-bedroom house gives a better return than a two-bedroom house (pound for pound), and a studio or one-bedroom flat attracts the wrong type of tenant in my area. Four-bedroom properties or above are okay for multi-letting, but this requires a high level of management that I do not want to be involved in on a long-term strategy.

- ROI or average net cashflow – this is crucial as it helps you to understand how many rooms are best suited to your strategy and whether it is buy and rent or multi-letting. Looking at the ROI figures lets you know how hard your money is working and whether or not this is a good use of that resource.

Once you have worked out your buying rules you can plan your second visit – this time knowing the property type, price and area you are looking for. You can test out your investment and see if you can find a property for your target tenant type, at the right price, that works for you or your client as an investment.

Take these buying rules (best kept in your head or note pad) and visit the estate agent contacts that you made on your last visit. Ask them for the sales details (the printed sheets) on properties they have available that fit your precise criteria (your property buying rules).

Don't arrange viewings yet. Go and visit the local letting agents and ask them for their opinion on your strategy. Show them the properties you have in your hand and, based on their comments, go back and arrange your viewings with the estate agents. Finally, go home and compare your new notes and numbers with all the information you have gathered to date, including the information from the earlier agent visits.

Letting agents

One other thing I would recommend you do while you are in the letting agent is obviously find out about their service and charges and effectively interview them as a potential business partner. Find out how they handle repairs and refurbishments. Do they use or recommend local builders? Do they have in-house staff?

Ask them questions such as how much will it cost to replace a bathroom, kitchen, decorate a property, fit a carpet or install central heating, etc? You can call a double-glazing company or two to get an idea on double-glazing costs. This will help you to build up a repairs and refurbishment schedule.

You will now have enough information to not only view the right property for your strategy in the right postcode, but you can start to calculate the ROI based on purchase price and refurbishment costs. You will also know the letting agent fees, cost of gas certificates, energy performance certificate (EPC) and tenant find fees. You have your investment model and can run the numbers to prove that it is a good deal for a client.

Chapter 8

Running the numbers – what makes a good deal?

You know what you expect to get from property investment and this is most likely cashflow (otherwise you would be reading another book!). You have carried out several days of desk research to narrow down your target investment areas. You have even been on location, 'got a feel for a place', met key future team members and now settled on *one* place. This is just the start…

I don't know where you will choose, but I do know that it will have hundreds of postcode areas (well, maybe not hundreds but certainly a lot). I have already suggested that you map out where different groups of people live (this sounds awful – sorry – but you need to understand the socio-geographic make-up of an area).

Next I am going to cover some of the actual maths to demonstrate, first, the difference between property prices and therefore areas and the impact on cashflow, and, second, the difference between property types and the impact on cashflow.

Before I do though, here is a brief recap on the impact numbers to consider:

1 ROTI – return on time invested

In Chapter 3 on page 51, I explained that understanding what your time is worth is critical in managing your time in a way that directs energy and effort towards balancing and increasing your cashflow. It can also help you to understand how much time a deal is worth. By this, I mean that if the deal is going to take lots of time to bring to the table, then I would want to be sure the returns are worth it. Remember my example of a coaching client who, prior to working with me, spent a year working on a deal to earn £200 per month.

So, if you have not already done so, calculate your hourly rate and as you work out the numbers and return on a deal think about whether you are going to be earning enough. Remember, the word 'enough' will be a different amount for each person and is based on your immediate and actual personal cashflow situation.

2 Yield

This is the first financial tool that you will use to narrow down your area, but it is very broad and does not help you to decide on a property type or specific location.

3 Below market valuation (BMV)

I have previously described this strategy as based on 'bulls*** values' because it requires a belief in fortune-telling, which is not a known business practice except at the funfair. What it does point to though is the importance of understanding what a valuation is and how to work it out. This is so *critical* as a skill that I will shortly discuss this point in some detail.

4 ROI

Understanding that the figures calculated by the ROI formulae are equivalent to interest earned on your money is vital in being able to evaluate deals and work out which deal is 'best value for money' or offers a better 'return' on your money – or that of a client. I focus on this topic on pages 131–134, repeating the formulae and using real case studies of deals, so that you can see what works and what doesn't. You can copy the formula yourself and a breakdown of the spreadsheet is available at TheSourcersApprentic.com.

Working out the true value of a property

We have all heard the words 'due diligence', but what do they really mean in the context of a property investment business? To me, the meaning comes in two parts.

First, the research that one puts in and continues to track about the area itself – what councils are planning, how government spending affects the plans for new roads or housing, the payment of benefits, the impact on social housing, prisoner release, vulnerable tenants or refugees.

Second, it comes down to the micro research carried out on a specific house that you are intending to buy or source for a client. That is what I want to focus on now because, if you guess an area but the numbers work on the property, you will make cashflow – for how long no one knows, but the deal will work. If you get the area right but buy the wrong property, you will definitely damage your cashflow potential and maybe even your long-term ability to hold the property. The key 'leveraging factor' about property investment is that you get the tenant to pay the mortgage. If there is no tenant or no rent, then you have to pay the mortgage or lose the property!

Alternatively, if you get the deal wrong and the rent does not cover the costs so there is no cashflow, then you are funding the mortgage. That is not leverage at all… in fact, that is not property investment. That is just buying lots of houses that you don't live in!

To value a property, many people will start with the sale price on Rightmove. This gives an indication of the *asking price*, which has no relationship whatsoever to the actual *sale price*. Actual sale price can be obtained through Land Registry or through certain sites like Mouseprice. However, it is already three months out of date at the point when you can access the information, simply because it takes Land Registry that long to update its data.

Value is determined by what you pay or are willing to pay for something and this is where I believe people get confused. Some prices are finite and non-negotiable, like your morning latte. Other items have negotiable prices like cars or art. There is a list or asking price and then, depending on your negotiation skills, there is a price that you will actually pay. You may even have that price in your head before you start the process, and that is a very good strategy to have. Other items, like foods nearing their best-before dates in a supermarket, are offered at a discount price because they need to be sold quickly or there is something wrong with the item – something has affected its perceived value.

So, if Rightmove displays the 'asking price' and that is not an indication of value or sale price, how do you work out the real value of a property? One easy way to do this is to 'employ' a local surveyor to talk you through their process – to teach you how they do it. I employed two local surveyors to survey a total of five properties (three properties each – one property was surveyed by both surveyors to check and compare their approaches and information).

I arranged that they would speak everything out loud to me rather than write a report. I learned about the local area in terms of geographical features (some areas have mines or Radon gas, others can be affected by subsidence or flooding), and the surveyors were an expert source. I learnt in one road that the flow of water during very heavy rain meant that all the basements on one side of the street flooded all winter. I learnt what cavity wall tie failure was and how it was treated. I learnt about damp-proof courses. The whole day cost me £500 and was worth every penny. Plus, I had five valuations and surveys.

I also learnt what surveyors consider as evidence of the value for a property and how they get comparisons. First, they look for sold prices, within three months, of like-for-like properties in the same road. If none exist, they might consider the road next to it, but local knowledge would tell you whether or not that was a true like-for-like comparison. One property I bought is worth £15,000 less than the road next door on a seemingly like-for-like comparison – similar structure and layout. Why? Because in the second road every house has a small open porch with a wrought-iron low fence and lattice work along the top of the porch. It makes the street look uniform and pretty and so more desirable; hence the difference in perceived and then actual value.

Top tips from surveyors

- Look at Rightmove to see the **asking price** for properties on sale in the road. If properties are being offered for less than your property, you will need to really understand why. Call the selling agent and ask about the property – even view it – it might be a better deal. It might have structural issues, be vandalised or be a repossession. (Repossessions are like 'creeping death' to the valuation of a street.)

- If one property is much **higher in valuation,** understand why. Most likely, the home owner has over extended and needs to clear the mortgage or has just got no idea! Know how long the property has been up for sale. On a road where I own a property, another carbon-copy house in a worse state of repair is on the market for £35,000 more than I paid for my property, and has been since the day I bought it in January 2009! The owners want to move to a new-build flat in town and need £100,000 to buy it.

- Now visit Mouseprice or similar sites like Nethouseprice and look for **sold properties.** Make sure you know whether the road has a mixed type of properties or just one property type. There is no point comparing a four-bedroom extended house to a two-bedroom original! Remember that properties in the same road (sold in the previous 3–4 months) would be considered a good comparable.

- If you have been working an area for some time, you will keep records of properties for sale in your area and know which agents sold them. You can then build or use your relationship with the estate agent to ascertain the actual sold prices much sooner than three months. As your **relationship with your estate agent** develops, you can ask them to check the Rightmove Professional site and tell you what has sold recently in the area you are looking at.

- **Know left from right.** There can be a big difference in house size, gardens and layout from one side of a street to another; ask your estate agent for some local knowledge.

- Finally, get on the phone. **Call local agents** and either:

  a) pretend you are looking to sell a property that great Auntie Flo has left you (be careful as I find this gets the sales people overexcited as they see a potential sale and so give you a higher valuation – you will have to explain 'quick sale' and 'offers in two weeks' to get them to lower their first valuation); or

  b) say you are looking for comps (comparisons or comparative prices) on XYZ properties, and hopefully they will tell you sold prices.

You will now have the following:

1. The asking price and an understanding of where your intended property sits in the range for that street and why.
2. The actual sold property prices that are three months old.
3. Possible sales, hot from the desk of your agent contacts.
4. An understanding of property types and differences on a street.
5. Comparables from local estate agents.

To calculate local values, I ignore the highest price and possibly the lowest if it appears as an anomaly – there are often reasons for these extremes. You will usually have a range, for example, between £45,000 (distressed repossession) and £100,000 (mad private seller) with a street value of around £70,000–£85,000.

Based on your knowledge gained through talking to estate agents, you will know whether the street is popular and a fast mover for sales (you will see higher priced property and they will be sold quickly) or a slower street. You will have driven up and down the road and the roads either side and opposite to give you a feel for it. You will have viewed the property itself and know its condition.

What you want to calculate, to the best of your ability, is what the property would sell for in a reasonable condition. On my streets, I would estimate a three-bedroom house with two reception rooms to sell for approximately £75,000 to £85,000, depending on postcode. I personally always take the lower value to be cautious, in this case £75,000. Then I deduct the cost of work and contingence to bring it up to standard of sale. So deducting another £7,500 brings the top purchase price to £67,500. This is not difficult. If you have a small area, then you will know your streets and your agents. You will already know the figure of £75,000 and then just need to deduct the cost of redecorating or a full refurbishment.

Offer price versus valuation

This is phase two. Okay, so in your head you know what the worse-case valuation is likely to be. You also know the asking price. Hopefully this is around your valuation figure, give or take 10–15%. Now what figure are you going to offer?

My offer price is already set. I know what price I want to pay – it is part of my buying rules. My rules 'tell me' the maximum price I want to pay for a two or three-bedroom property because I want to achieve a certain cashflow and, therefore, can only afford to pay a certain price. (You will see this in the examples on page 120.)

So, if my rules state that my top price for a three-bedroom property (including any refurbishment costs) is £65,000, for example, and the asking price is £75,000, then I would make an offer of £65,000 less the refurbishment costs of £7,500 – meaning an offer of £57,500. You might wonder why I have 'deducted' the refurbishment costs twice. There are two reasons: first, if the house needs the work, then in my opinion it is not worth the 'normal' price; second, having worked out what I want to pay (£65,000), I then need to deduct any refurbishment costs. If the asking price was £85,000, then I would have to know more about the 'story' of the seller to understand how to negotiate.

Making an offer

I am very honest with my estate agent contacts. When I arrive to view properties or call to arrange them, I let them know how many properties I want to buy and will casually mention if I am doing viewings with another agent. That way the estate agent knows the situation. Ultimately, it is all about making it easy for them to make a sale – not to waste their time.

Once I have viewed properties I will give the estate agents some immediate feedback, such as 'I like that' or 'OMG are you serious?' I will flag up 2–4 potential deals out of the 8–12 I have viewed that day (not necessarily all with one agent). I will let them know I am going to check some figures and then email or call them within 48 hours (depends where we are in the week).

That evening I will enter all my property data into my part-prepared spreadsheet. I already know the area value and rental income, so now I can add in the refurbishment costs and the asking price. From the spreadsheet, I can see what cashflow and ROI any given asking price would return.

If I hit my target cashflow, I would then be negotiating a purchase price just to get the best possible deal. If, when I enter the numbers, the cashflow is poor, then I know I need to offer a lower price. I use the spreadsheet to calculate this and I will reduce the offer price figure until I hit over £250 per month net cashflow, or an ROI over 10% - then I know how low I would have to go!

I will have already asked the estate agent the following questions:

- Who is the vendor? Is it a private sale (which can be expensive) or a probate sale (they can be greedy)? What about the landlord (often they can be over stretched)? Or is it a repossession (which is fixed price and very structured)?

- When did the property come to the market? (If it's early days, then the vendor is unlikely to accept an offer. You can still make one, but just don't be surprise if the answer is 'No'.)

- How many viewings have there been? (If there have been lots and no offers, there is often a story here – there is either something wrong with the house or vendor!)

- How many offers have there been? (As above, there can be a story here.)

- I then always ask (maybe because I have a good relationship with the agents) what is the lowest offer that the vendor is prepared to accept? This gives me a guide – I don't always stick to it though.

Sometimes I let the estate agent know my workings out and why a deal just won't work for me. They can give feedback to a vendor and sometimes the asking price is reduced. Often the property stays on the market at the asking price for ages until the vendor reaches that desperate trigger and accepts an offer. If too many months have passed, my offer will often have reduced further.

Typical examples of offers I would make are shown on page 134. Generally, they are around my maximum purchase price rule or lower. I don't bother to calculate my offer based on a percentage of asking price, as I found that it gave me a false figure to work on. This was because if I estimated the street value wrong and then offered 25% below it, I might still be above my buying rule. I offer a price in order to get the cashflow; after all, I want this to be a long-lasting successful business!

Rules and gut instinct

I do operate a lot of my business now based on instinct; it's a bit like riding a bike and feeling your balance. When I first started it was very much by these rules:

1. Know my street values.
2. Know my buying rules – maximum purchase price I am willing to pay to get my target cashflow.
3. Build my relationship with my estate agent and know how to speak to them.

Start by using your rules and stick to them. As you get a feel for them and the area you are working in, you can start to bend, expand and reshape the rules and test out where the breaking point is. Find out where the deal breaker is and then operate below that line. When I say 'test out', do so simply by expanding the range of properties you view not by actually buying them!

ROI examples

If you look at the examples on page 134, you will see that I have compared a three-bedroom house with a two-bedroom flat and a HMO. I have also compared the north of England and London. Let's start with the noticeable differences in property types.

First, flats have an additional service charge for the overall maintenance of communal areas of the property – you will still need to maintain the inside of your own property. Depending on the state of the management accounts and the quality of the property, this can be a costly expense that you have no control over.

In 2009, one of my original London flats fell due for a seven-year major works repair schedule – it cost the block over £8m and my share was £8,500. This was for a coat of paint on an external balcony and windows (not new windows) and repairs to the flat roof (not a new roof). Thank goodness interest rates fell, as this was over £630 per month from my net rent, on top of lift repairs (£100) and a new door entry system (£98). I had no say or control over this work – it was carried out in accordance with the lease by the freeholder! Luckily the property still cashflowed at the end of it.

The second comparison is with the HMO. You need to be clear on the tenant type you are planning to attract as, whilst this may be obvious, a number of strangers will have to live under one roof with one or two bathrooms and one kitchen. Often when the tenant type is LHA, the only people who would live in shared accommodation are single males. With new changes from 2012, this will extend to everyone under 35. Of course many single girls soon get babies and then 'earn' more benefits and can afford flats or houses. Single males (long-term single males) usually come with challenges like drug or alcohol abuse. Please don't write and accuse me of stereotyping – I do understand that everyone is different – I am just explaining what I discovered when I considered this option in my area.

HMOs in city centres or on transport links near universities or hospitals could attract working or student tenants, each coming with their own challenges. Students, by nature of their courses, work to a specific timetable. Complete on a property in December and it may not get a new batch of students until the following September – how are you going to budget for this? There can be higher refurbishment costs in between rental periods – have you budgeted for this?

Lastly, HMOs usually require the landlord to pay the bills – these costs are often included in the rent. The consequence for you is that those additional costs are coming out of your profit. Tenants do not see the bills and do not necessarily conserve energy as we might at home. Make sure you budget adequately for HMO utility bill costs; they certainly bring down the profit margin.

When you compare the actual cashflow £308 and £601 respectively, they are the highest on the table. However, if you consider how much more it costs to 'buy' the investment, your ROI is just 6% – considerably less.

Now let's consider the area. When you look at the gross rent possible on a West London three-bedroom house, you are talking about £1,200 – over double the rent in the north. However, the prices reflect this and when you consider the amount of money needed to 'buy' the investment compared to the rent, using ROI you can see that you get a better return further north.

In fact, you actually get better cashflow too. If you consider the £80,795 you would need to spend to buy a property in London, you could buy three properties up north costing £26,364 each, and earn a combined net rent off all three properties of £901.50 – a considerably better cashflow.

Using ROI as a measure to compare deals you can see why I moved my personal investment strategy from close to home to further north, where the purchase price and rental ratios work better. I did still set out on that first trip to look at student HMOs as I thought they offered better cashflow, but soon realised that I could get better cashflow (easier management) and 'any time' renting by focusing on traditional buy-to-let property and ASTs.

Look at the spreadsheet on page 134. Replicate the formulae (check out TheSourcersApprentice.com if you'd like a copy) and then start experimenting with property costs and potential rental income and see what you discover.

Narrowing down your search

Now that you understand ROI and how relatively simple the spreadsheet is, you can start to look at your area in more detail. Start looking at postcode areas. What is the difference in ROI between A1 B23 and Z1 Y23? What is the difference in social class, building type, access routes, schools, commercial and then rents and purchase prices?

How the numbers work: real case studies of deals

Property	West London house	North West house	North West flat	North West HMO	West London HMO
Number of beds	3	3	2	5	5
Market rent	1,200.00	550.00	490.00	900.00	1,875.00
Asking price	270,000.00	75,000.00	70,000.00	150,000.00	320,000.00
My estimation	255,000.00	65,000.00	60,000.00	145,000.00	315,000.00
Offer price	255,000.00	61,500.00	55,000.00	145,000.00	315,000.00
75% mortgage (or 70% HMO)	191,250.00	46,125.00	41,250.00	101,500.00	220,500.00
Mortgage rate	0.048	0.048	0.048	0.054	0.054
Cost of mortgage	765.00	184.50	165.00	456.75	992.25
Costs to rent					
Monthly property insurance	18.00	10.00	-	-	-
Letting agent fee 10% or 15%	120.00	55.00	49.00	135.00	281.25
Service charges	-	-	55.00	-	-
Utility bills	-	-	-	125.00	175.00
Net rent	297.00	300.50	276.00	308.25	601.50
Costs to buy					
Cost of deposit (25% or 30%)	63,750.00	15,375.00	13,750.00	43,500.00	94,500.00
Solicitor costs & disb	1,100.00	1,100.00	1,100.00	1,100.00	1,100.00
Broker and survey	650.00	650.00	650.00	650.00	650.00
Certificates (gas, EPC)	165.00	125.00	125.00	125.00	165.00
Tenant find	600.00	245.00	245.00	245.00	937.50
8 weeks void allowance	1,530.00	369.00	330.00	913.50	1,984.50
Portfolio management fee	5,500.00	5,500.00	5,500.00	5,500.00	5,500.00
Refurbishment budget	7,500.00	3,000.00	2,500.00	10,000.00	12,500.00
Cash required to buy	80,795.00	26,364.00	24,200.00	62,033.50	117,337.00
Return on investment (ROI)	0.04	0.14	0.14	0.06	0.06
Yield	0.06	0.11	0.11	0.07	0.07
	Near university & hospital	LHA family	LHA family	Unemployed men with alcohol or drug issues	Near university & hospital

You will start to narrow down a small group of postcodes, which in larger towns and cities will often be found on the outer circular road (there's always a ring road or boundary road of some sort). Look at Birmingham, Manchester, Rotherham, Stoke, Margate, Essex, Grimsby or Hull. You can even find sections of London that hold true. Once you have decided on 2–3 main postcode areas in your chosen town or city, go to another level of detail and start to find the specific streets that you favour.

Building relationships – the foundation to success

All the professionals I have mentioned: estate agents and letting agents, the build teams, insurance brokers, mortgage brokers and solicitors are a vital part of your team. Okay, that is obvious – maybe what we forget is what they want to achieve in the relationship and how they want to be treated.

I would still suggest that you effectively interview every one of them – you don't need to tell them that this is what you are doing though. Just engage them in conversation, knowing in advance that you are looking for key service deliverables.

I would create a job description for your ideal letting agent and estate agent, your ideal builder or broker and then as you speak to them score them against your criteria. Of course, you could just go on gut instinct. I still do that a great deal. The other 'choice' factor is a referral by someone you trust.

Build a relationship. Remember you are one of many people who they have to deal with. Remember to say thank you in words or small tokens. I take a bottle of wine and chocolates to my estate agent every time I complete on a deal. I invite them to dinner a couple of times a year.

Each member of my team is a business in their own right, but they are also a person who I actually like and so have conversations and remember important details about them.

What personality type are you?

You might be a really detailed person; you might be a 'people and feelings' orientated person. Think about your personality type. How do you like to receive information? Do you like pictures or do you prefer things to be written down? Do you text or call? Do you want the facts quickly or would you like to get to know me first?

Once you understand the person and personality type you are, you can start to be more aware of the people you speak to. Yes, if you understand how to create rapport, then do so, but be congruent. I certainly wouldn't even attempt a conversation about football or cars. My only connections to football or cars are an *Everything a girl needs to know about football* book (a gift from my daughter's boyfriend still on my 'to read' list) and a Nissan Micra (which is red and really I wanted a light green one but they didn't have any left!)

I have recognised that people glaze over when I start spouting numbers or go into too much detail. I also speak quickly and have conversations that go off on tangents, as I think of new thoughts. You might have noticed that trait in this book too! Now when speaking to new people I aim to breathe deeply, speak more slowly, be clear about what I want to achieve and be conscious of the signs they are giving off in terms of interest level or their own congruency.

As you move around the country, you will find people with different interests and priorities. Be sensitive to these among your potential team and among potential vendors. You might need to be brave as you first start out and ask questions. I believe that it is in our human nature to help, unless you catch a person at month-end when targets are not met and they are busy completing their commission statement!

I would counsel against walking into an estate agent and asking for a 30% discount on a property when you have no cash or clients. Build up to it. However, if it does all go horribly wrong, there is always another estate agent, letting agent, broker or even town.

Chapter 9

Understanding the service you are offering

At this point some of you will be bursting to go and buy the deals that you have discovered. If you have the cash to invest, great, off you go. However, I would still suggest that before you buy for yourself, you think through what you are specifically doing and how it can be of interest to other potential cash-rich clients.

If you want to buy cashflowing buy-to-let properties and either you are new to investing, have no personal cash to invest or have invested in the past but your money is tied up so you are looking for a new strategy – this is the chapter for you.

Think about the product you have: cashflow, cash flowing investment packages, a business opportunity for someone with cash sitting in a bank, building society or property. You can, for a fee, introduce them to (or sell them) the deal. This all sounds great, but in order to communicate the message of the opportunity you have, you need to be able to describe it in a way that would attract the people (clients) you are looking for. What problem are you solving for your client?

Think about who would want a cashflowing deal. If you are just going to sell the deal on its own, who would have the skills and contacts to successfully complete the purchase without your help? Personally, I am too much of a control freak to leave the completion, and therefore the success or failure of a deal, in someone else's hands! I recognised quite early on that if I only got paid on completion, then I had to make sure that completion occurred; otherwise I was working for nothing.

So I believe what I have is a 'service'. I help (project manage) people with cash to invest in cashflow property investments. When I think about who they are, what they do, what they know – I can then start to think about what interests them and therefore how to talk to them.

Who are your clients going to be? What sort of a 'sourcing' service do they need? What skills do they already possess and what do they need you to do for them? Now you can start to describe your 'ideal' client, you can start to describe the service they want (not what you want to offer – what *they* want!) You can also start to think about your cashflowing deals and how you can describe these to them in a way that meets their information needs and solves their problem.

I learnt that this tied in very closely with the point I made in Chapter 8 on page 136 about knowing yourself. Do you talk about detail? Do you skim over detail? What does your client need? In my experience, I certainly gave too much information at the start – I almost overwhelmed my clients with facts, figures, details and images. I made it impossible for them to decide.

I knew that my clients did not have a lot of time or specific knowledge about the details of property investment, hence they needed my services. I originally thought that if I gave them all of the information I had gathered to decide that a deal was right for them as an investment, that I would save them time and give them reassurance. All I gave most clients was a headache and a near-impossible decision to make. Fortunately, most of my early clients were not into detail, so didn't read the stuff I sent them anyway!

I have now trimmed down all the detail of the information I share with clients to the bare minimum facts they need to know:

- Offer price;

- Monthly cashflow;

- Cash required to invest;

- ROI; and

- A brief description of the house (mid terrace, three bedrooms, two reception rooms).

Once one of my clients decides, on that basis, that they either want to invest or have more information, then I can provide it immediately because I had it all along – I just need to give it to them in smaller chunks. On a first deal, most clients will want more information. However, as they start to recognise the benefit of the deals that you source for them, they will probably require less information.

I have one client who has had minimal information from me, seen no photos and only visited the area 18 months after the first purchase. They have bought four properties with me. I have another client who said they did not want the detail and then repeatedly became anxious just before and during the purchase phase, because actually they do not want the detail but they *need* it! It's just that work commitments kept them so busy. I have another client who read every word of the purchasing contract and noticed that page 109 was missing when it was faxed over to them by the solicitor!

Work with your clients – have all the information ready and provide it as required by each client and their desire for detail, reassurance or time. Remember, it is your responsibility to present the best possible deal available at that moment in time. It is the client's responsibility to decide whether or not they want to invest and they need to carry out their own due diligence – they need to be responsible for spending their own money!

So what sort of service are you going to offer?

This may be decided by the contacts you have in an area; it may be decided by whether or not you are working full time. Ultimately, the question is how far through the purchasing and tenanting process will you be supporting your client?

You could:

* Introduce the deal and then stand back;
* Introduce the deal and support through to completion;

- Support through to completion and project manage the refurbishment process; or

- Support completion, refurbishment and tenant find.

There is no right or wrong answer. I think it is a matter of:

- Time – how much do you have?

- Contacts – do you have any?

- Passion – do you enjoy this?

If you don't already invest in an area and have not been involved in the refurbishment of properties before, then you could keep it simple to start with. You could just find the deals, supply a list of local agents that could manage a refurbishment, simply introduce your client to the 3–4 letting agents you recommend and then duck out of the process at completion. It will certainly take less of your time, which means you can move on to your next deal more quickly. I would ask you though to consider the question of whether your clients can then take that property and make it cashflow, because without cashflow they won't see, feel and experience the real benefits of the investment opportunity.

If you already invest or plan to invest in an area, or if you are more confident about refurbishments, then maybe you would prefer to project manage more of the process. This will impact on how much you charge.

How much to charge

This is where you can fall back on your hourly rate and consider how long it will take you to find, negotiate, complete, refurbish and support through to tenancy, a complete property investment deal. Then the number of hours or days multiplied by your rate will give you an idea of a chargeable fee.

You may still want to offer a discounted rate to start with in order to attract clients and build your reputation. You may want to check out what others in the market or your area are offering. Remember, your rate is based on your service, your knowledge and expertise and, above all, your hourly rate based on your financial needs. So checking another person's rate is a benchmark, not an absolute piece of information.

It was only a matter of months before I realised that I had more deals than I could buy. However, I knew that I had the skills, contacts and track record to sell these on and so my sourcing business was borne. I did, of course, 'faff' around for another three months before I actually offered a deal to anyone. I was stepping up my game. Initially I had the courage to buy for me and then my family, but now I was going to share my investment ideas with strangers. What if they knew more than me? What if they didn't like the deal? What if they asked a question I didn't know the answer to?

All of these fears are natural. However, they also constitute an expectation of a negative outcoume that may not be realised!:

1. If a client knows more than you, great. This is an opportunity to learn. They will be experienced, have properties already and you could work closely and grow your mutual businesses.
2. If they don't like the deal, that is fine – they don't have to buy it. Other investors will like the deal – think how to explain it and get to the point a lot quicker.
3. What if they ask a question you don't know the answer to? Then you would say that you will find out. People don't see honesty as a weakness, well nice people don't.

This business is all about relationships and communication skills and you can learn to get better at both, if you need to.

So how much should you charge? My answer is that it depends on what you do. As part of your research, speak to other sourcing agents in the market. See how they present their deals and how much they charge their clients, bearing in mind this will still only be a benchmark. There is a massive price range depending on the service that is provided:

- Lead generation – website generated – unqualified leads sell for £5–£25.

- Lead generated and part-qualified contacts can sell for £25–£100.

- Packaged deals – this has implied no money down (NMD) deals in the past, where clients pay £5,000–£7,000 and the dealer is often making a cut on the property price and sometimes property management. The client will have a 100% mortgage, no equity and little (even *negative*) cashflow.

- Packaged deals – where the sourcing agent charges a fee (£5–£7,000) for sourcing and then retains a share in the property's future capital growth. (This feels like having your cake and eating it too, but some clients are happy to pay for this, which seems like a lot of money to me.)

- Source up to completion for £2,500–£7,000 – in London some people charge a percentage fee of 1–3%.

- Source up to tenancy. Again, either for a fee or a percentage like above.

Whatever you charge it has to work in the deal. There still has to be great cashflow for the client and, of course, the all important ROI. Looking at the spreadsheet on page 134, you can see I charge £5,500 for a deal taken through completion, refurbishment to tenanting. I have considered how much time it takes. I have considered my contacts and my track record. I have considered value for money and ROI.

My deals offer great cashflow and ROI for people who work and are dissatisfied with the current returns they are achieving. Some recognise the untapped resources they have at hand; some clients are retired or just buy outright for cash.

What about finding investor clients?

I know that there are so many people out there with money invested in the stock market, sitting in savings accounts, lying dormant in property, that really there is no reason not to find a client. I think it comes down to confidence, understanding your service and explaining the deal in a way that your prospective client wants to receive the information.

It also means developing a thick skin (note to self) and not to take rejection personally! Remember that, although you have found a way to become financially secure, possibly even financially free in a few years time, some people, especially those trained at school and/or in jobs, need structure, need to work and may even fear change.

Some of your clients are working through an internal battle; they recognise that things need to change but maybe they fear getting it wrong, or simply listen to the news too much – that's okay – that's for them to resolve when they are ready. So, if they say no to a deal, it is not 'no' to you, it's, 'No I am *not ready* to make this change yet!' Your job is to share the opportunity with people – when they are ready they will come to you.

In 2010, I started to change where I spent the bulk of my 'networking' time. I wanted to go somewhere where I felt supported to grow my business. I stopped going to property networking events in October 2010, unless I had been invited to speak. I went back to a business group that I had been a part of since 2007, though not actively contributing to for over 18 months.

Ecademy is an online and offline network that combines 'Facebook socialising' with 'LinkedIn business focus' and a lot of local business networking groups like NRG or BNI, but without the compulsion to promote others. Ecademy started with founder Penny Power's belief of 'Know Me, Like Me, Follow Me'. People like people and mostly want to help. It was just what I needed.

As I sat there at our Christmas party on a table full of men, I found that I was in my element. One guest commented that he had £800,000 sitting in his account; another asked me what I would do if he gave me £1million. My little voice immediately wanted to crack a joke about buying an around-the-world ticket to go scuba diving. Luckily, I realised this question was half serious. I replied, 'It depends on whether you are looking for long-term investment returns or short-term gains. In the short term, I could probably offer 6–8% return' (never start too high), 'however in the longer term you could be looking at anywhere between 10–25% ROI, depending on your attitude towards the investments' (never mention risk).

The man nodded and made an 'mmm' sound. It had fallen silent on the table as everyone listened and then all of a sudden conversation picked up. A friend next to me lent over and whispered, 'He is just selling his multimillion pound business – he owns his own helicopter and a fleet of rare cars!' That's when I knew that people with money look just like us, just like my parents, my neighbour or the person in the shopping queue! Don't judge – speak. Just talk to people. In fact, even better – have a conversation and ask questions. I met the same man again recently and we are going to renew our conversation!

Ask questions with care

I remember one of my coaches saying that 'the person who asks the most questions, controls the conversation'. It is definitely a skill that can be learnt. 'Be interested not interesting!' There is a balance to be struck between drilling someone mercilessly for information and having a conversation that has an underlying fact-finding purpose. It can be as simple as setting an intention or goal for the conversation to remind you of what you would like to know.

'Do you have any money to invest?' is not the best way to start! 'How would you like to take this forward?' can be a good way to end.

People like to talk about themselves – crikey I do, although I am getting boring now as I have heard a lot of what I have to say before! Give other people a chance to talk about their hopes and dreams – what they like and what they want. Some will want to talk about what they don't like and what they don't want. It takes all sorts.

Establishing the relationship

If we don't speak to one another, we can't build a relationship with one another. How do you move from having a conversation to building an investment relationship? You ask the question.

It depends what is being said in the conversation, but there is always a point where you can ask the question, 'Is that something you want to move forward on? Or... explore? Or.... discuss?' How about, 'What do you need to know now to make a decision?' You may not take the opportunity, because *you* are not ready, or you may pick up the vibe that the other person is not ready (which may or may not be accurate).

If you don't ask, you definitely don't get. It's as simple as that. If you don't ask someone if they want to talk to you about how you can use your skills and knowledge to help them achieve what they want in life, then you are denying them the opportunity you have – you are selfish!

After a series of shorter conversations (often networking at events or via email) a potential client will decide that they want to know how they can move forward. How long it takes the client to make this decision differs for everyone. We then usually have about a half hour conversation, which is really an opportunity for them to tell me what help they want. Depending on their circumstances, I will either help them to make money from their property knowledge through a mentorship or coaching, or meet them to start the process of 'shopping for houses'.

Getting to know the client

There will be lots of ways to do this. My preferred way – because it's my way – is to have a formal strategy session where we meet privately and work out what the client wants to achieve, in fact, everything that I have described in this book.

I take them through a five-step process, which culminates in a personalised investment action plan and the possibility of our working together. I understand where they are financially, what they want to achieve, and I know whether my model will work for them. For some, it does not and it's really important that one of you finds this out very early on! This is not a sales opportunity particularly – it is a personalised strategy development session that leaves my clients better informed and clearer about their objectives and opportunities.

I usually buy 'stinky houses', and I call them that because they often have damp – usually from a leaking gutter – or they smell dirty or empty. They will mostly have been repossessed and left in a poor condition for some 6–12 months while the repossession process moved through the courts. I buy houses because I still want the opportunity to circulate my money, and that of clients, through an optional remortgage after 12 months.

I have a client who did not like the sound of stinky houses – even though that is where the cash is! They needed more security. They already had a portfolio that was in negative cashflow. So I explained different types of investment opportunities to them.

I can also, for specific cash-rich clients, access renovated HMOs on long leases with all inclusive bills and management fees. This specific product needs to be bought for cash and then remortgaged after six months or bought with commercial mortgages. My builder identifies certain geographically located properties for a specific price and then fully renovates them to order. That was what they wanted. The client needed the security of a longer lease and 'guaranteed' cashflow to off-set the negative cashflow. They wanted a clean and tidy house to start with. We are now in the process of buying two properties for them with 15–23% net ROI after the six month remortgage.

I will say it once again: if your service does not meet your client's needs, then you must find out and be clear about it. Refer them to someone else. Build referral relationships. The client may need to develop their personal financial strategy or mindset – give them a copy of this book!

Turning it on its head – the property comes first

Just to turn this on its head for a moment, I have been talking mostly about my model, which is based on my service. I also buy cashflowing properties in the north with the intention of holding on to them for the long term, during which time I will carry out one remortgage, at roughly the one-year stage, to release the bulk of my cash investment – more if I can.

One of my business partners works the model the other way round and that is how we complement one another. They find deals in London for clients who are looking for potential capital growth. Then they offer the deal to their database, and then charge a percentage fee.

The difference is that I only look at property I intend to buy either for myself or a client, while they find deals and then offer them to a wider group, who may or may not be in a position to buy the deal at that time.

What do you want to become?

- An area specialist?

- A strategy specialist?

- A deal finder?

Or offer your working model?

Chapter 10

The contract and the paperwork

Think of your contract document as a 'process document' that explains to your clients exactly what you will do on their behalf and where their responsibility in the process starts and finishes. Don't consider it as a legal document to pursue someone in court; however, it should be detailed and may contain legal jargon.

Whether you buy a ready-made contract or create your own, I guarantee that you will redevelop it as your experience with clients increases. Initially, I only took payments on completion and then realised that clients could go part of the way through the process with me and then change their mind. I would not get paid for the research and time I had already spent!

I also recognised that in my sourcing business model, I was using contacts that I needed for my own portfolio development – they are really important to me. If a client pulled out after initially saying yes to a deal, that would damage my reputation and my relationship! I added in clauses that required stage payments for the work I was carrying out on behalf of clients. It also stated that if a client just 'changed' their mind, then there was a no-refund policy.

How you get paid – what you get paid for

Think through your process, understand the steps involved and the actions that you need your client to take. Write them down and maybe pass them to a friend to read through to check they make sense.

As you write down the stages of your buying process, think about what could go wrong at each stage, what it would have cost you to get to that stage and what you can do next. Let's think through a buying process:

1. As you carry out your research and search for a deal, there are costs such as travel and your time spent viewing the deals to be considered. Do you want to be paid for this? If so, how much? Now consider why the client would pay you for this – what are they paying for and what happens if you don't find anything?
2. So you have found a deal, how much information do you give the client straight away? Do they need to pay for this? If so, how much and why? What if they don't like the deal? What then?
3. They agree to buy – what now? I would assume that you might go ahead and negotiate a bit harder on the deal, maybe speak to a broker or solicitor. How much time will you spend? When will you be paid for this?
4. What happens if your client can't get a mortgage? What happens if the survey is bad or worse than expected?
5. How do you ensure that you get paid on completion?
6. What if it all goes wrong?

In a way, the development of your contract is like a risk analysis for your business. With a property deal you might consider the risk factors, the level of risk and everything you can do to mitigate those risks. The same is true with the client process; think through the steps, then consider what could go wrong, the level of risk of that happening and what the consequences (and costs) are to you. Lastly, think how you can mitigate the risks to an acceptable level.

For example, I used to give my clients the full postal code and access to all due diligence for a property upfront – in the days when I gave too much information, too much detail. One client asked to visit the property so that meant they had my agent details as well. This enabled them to go direct to my contact and cut me out of the deal. The client decided not to go ahead, which is their right. I had not been paid for two trips to view the property, my time negotiating the deal and arranging the visits and I had even incurred overnight expenses in a hotel. The issue being that I had not asked for any payment upfront. I may have been paid nothing but I did learn a valuable lesson.

If a client wants to view a property, I manage the process through my contract to ensure that I am fairly paid for research and contacts that I have made on a client's behalf.

Another client who did buy through me is now in direct contact with my agent to buy another property. Could I mitigate against this by putting in my contract that any future properties bought in the same area without my help would result in a £500 fee, or something to that effect? Would I put effort into enforcing it? I don't know! If a client does not recognise the value that you offer, that is a matter for their time and not your attention!

So now that you have a list of the stages of your business model, you will understand (as much as you can at this time) about what might go wrong and what you can do about it. You will even understand where your costs are in the process. This will give you your payment schedule. Whether or not you choose to ask for staged payments is entirely up to you and the level of your service. If you are just selling unqualified leads, then payment is full and final.

This time, I have not put a list here deliberately. Not because I don't want to share this information, but because I want you to think about your own personal business model rather than mine.

My model works for me, my lifestyle, my contacts, my knowledge and skill. You must be comfortable with the service that you are going to offer, especially if you are going to charge people money for it. I hope that makes sense. We do cover this in much more detail in our sourcing resource called *The Sourcer's Apprentice* and you can find more information at TheSourcersApprentice.com.

Making the deal secure

If you have spoken with your client, understood their needs and know that you can fulfil them, then you have a relationship. The contract lays out the terms and conditions, and also serves as another way of explaining exactly what you are going to do. As part of that explanation, you might ask for staged payments. As you present your contract to your client, you should have effectively secured your deal to the best of your ability. Remember, though, there is 'nowt as strange as folk'. Not everyone will share your business values or ethics.

Additional security comes in the form of your relationship with your estate agent, broker, solicitor and letting agent. If clients bypass you, it just means you did a good job. If they now want to use their own time travelling to the area, negotiating deals, then fine, you have plenty of other clients to work with – move on. You are busy doing it all again for another client or one of your existing clients who does value your time and the service you offer, someone who recognises that by leveraging your time they can spend their time doing other things.

What if it all goes wrong?

I suppose it depends on what you mean by 'all goes wrong'! To start with, you have written down your process, which means you understand what you are doing (to the best of your ability); you have considered the risks and looked to mitigate your expenses and protect your reputation through terms in the contract. If a client chooses not to buy or can't get a mortgage, then move on – you know the steps to take. Nothing is personal and challenges are just lessons spelt differently.

What *not* to do

Do nothing

If you do nothing, you will learn nothing – earn nothing – change nothing. Whatever you do, do it consciously – with purpose – and understand as many of the consequences as you can. Remember that as emotion goes up, intelligence goes down, and that is why you need to think and plan and do. Do something; whatever happens you will learn from it.

Make an offer you can't follow through on

This, for me, is fundamental. I only make an offer (in Scotland this would constitute a binding verbal contract) that I know – to the best of my ability – I can fulfil. Making an offer you can't follow through on lets down the vendor and the estate agent. Ultimately it will damage your reputation.

Panic or put your head in the sand

- If a client pulls out, find out why and resolve it.

- If a property falls through, find out why and resolve it.

- If an estate agent sells a property to someone else, find out why and refine the relationship.

Keep the estate agents, vendors, brokers, solicitors and builders informed as necessary. If you ignore a challenge or a problem, it will only get worse.

Doing it all again – moving on to the next level

At this stage, I thought I would combine 'doing it all again' with talking about moving on to the next level of business, as some of you will have already been sourcing deals and may not have thought of yourselves as running a business.

If you are already sourcing, then hopefully the last few sections will have taken you through a thought process that is already making you think about how you can develop your business. Now I want to talk about business growth.

There are two key factors in business growth: first, having the time to grow your business and, second, the systems in place to give you the time. Ironically, you may need the time to develop the systems that will then give you the time to grow your business!

Depending on your current position, you can pick and choose your way through the next few sections, but ultimately you will need to work through all of them if you want to increase your personal cashflow, grow your personal portfolio and eventually retire early.

Outsourcing

This does not have to be directly associated with your sourcing business. If you already own a property portfolio, this might mean employing a letting agent instead of self-managing, or handing over maintenance, refurbishments and repairs to another company. Now before you start arguing about how only you can do it and the cost of outsourcing, think back to Chapter 3, page 48 explaining time and ROTI. If you are still not convinced, then let's work through this exercise quickly.

I guarantee that whatever counter argument you come up with to justify why you don't need to outsource, I have already argued that myself. I effectively delayed the growth of my own business by at least a year if not 18 months. With hindsight, I can accept that it was for the right reason and it has worked perfectly for me, but at least acknowledge that you haven't yet outsourced because you are not ready (for whatever reason) and save yourself the constant merry-go-round. Either outsource or don't – the choice is yours – but you won't grow easily or as quickly without.

Where to start?

Record all your activities and how long they take you (I suggested this in Section 1) and then use your hourly rate to work out how much they cost you. I bet that you can buy (outsource) them for a cheaper hourly rate. Take, for example, my cleaner. She costs £8 per hour. I know that I can earn more than that in an hour. The trick to making outsourcing work for you is to actually work and earn money while the cleaner is doing the hoovering!

If you find the idea of outsourcing daunting, trust me I am right there with you. As I mentioned, it took me 18 months to actually outsource work successfully. I tried two friends and then finally went to a professional! Get in touch and I will happily recommend to you the virtual assistants (VAs) I know. One runs a brilliant consultancy service, where she helps you outsource the process of outsourcing. In the space of a three-hour meeting, she understood what I did in a day, which tasks she could routinise for me and which tasks I could teach her to take over. We then identified the core essential activities that I had to do myself. Ultimately, almost everything I do can be routinised.

So once you have discovered your non-essential, non-urgent tasks (eg. filing) and your essential, routine tasks (eg. monitoring AST, gas certificates and rent), you can outsource them and then use that time to map out your systems with a view to creating a property administrator role. What things could someone carry out if they followed your precise instructions?

With your extra time and newly-discovered systems, you will have more time to do the bit that only you or your business partner can do, and really that is talking to clients. Everything else can be outsourced. As a part of my service, I guarantee my clients that I will view every property inside and out myself. Maybe in future years I will choose to change that. Think about your service and what you are offering.

A brief word about systems

If you are an 'action taker', I imagine you will already be rushing to turn the pages – you don't want to think about, let alone read about, systems. BUT this is where money can be made. Not just in the sale of your systems, but more fundamentally in the development of your business.

By working through the systems you employ to find a deal, you can identify ways to improve and enhance your service and effectively increase your hourly rate. My original deal analysis spreadsheet was so detailed and complex that it took a week to enter and qualify the 12 deals that I had viewed in one day! I ran every scenario; I was double-checking and that was good in the early stages, but I actually took so long I lost some of the better deals because other investors put offers in before me!

The spreadsheet had beautifully coloured and designed boxes, each stage or option would print out perfectly. My spreadsheet now is a simple document containing only the key information of the primary strategy. I do not need a detailed analysis of every 'what if'; I just need to know that *if* 'what if' happens, I can work it out *if* needed! My new simple, black and white spreadsheet is completed in approximately an hour, depending on how many properties I have seen and how legible my handwritten notes are. I can then sort it, edit it and send it direct to my client.

Property management systems

The second area to consider is the property management system for your own portfolio. If you are using a letting agent, how do you monitor and manage the information flow on your current portfolio? Is stuff in your diary or in your head? Is it written down so someone else can do it for you or under your control because it is so important? 'Write it down', 'use a diary system' and 'use someone else' are actually the right answers to the questions above.

Do you remember how I spoke about the example of the glass that is 80% full in Chapter 4 on page 71, which meant that you are stressed? That 'need' to create space is what this section is all about. Without space you cannot grow your business.

Ideally, you need to spend your time building relationships with clients who you can sell property deals to. Could you focus on working with, say, six active clients at a time, which would mean finding one deal per week and completing roughly every six weeks? You could make £5,000 per working week, take eight weeks off a year for holidays, fun and personal development and still make in excess of £220,000 per annum. Less 40% tax (not counting expenses) would be £132,000 – is that enough? Is it worth giving your attention to systems and outsourcing?

Reputation and marketing

Once you have your systems in place and you have outsourced the non-essential tasks, you can focus on growing your business. How do you do this? Well, one easy way is to talk to more people – what if you could get people who were interested in property investment to come and find you, to want to speak to you and make themselves known to you?

This is where marketing comes in. I am not going to claim to be an expert marketeer – there are plenty of those out there. What I would rather do is, again, raise some questions for you to think about before you spend any money.

Who...? What...?

- Who is your client?

- What do they do now?

- What are they interested in?

- What are the problems that you can solve for them?

This is like marketing 101 – but maybe it is even more important to think about this now that we have a 'social media and global network'. There are so many dimensions in which we can communicate with one another – from the traditional 'just speaking to people' (but then you have to know which event to attend and who out of the 50–1,000 people to speak to) to a more massive media-enabled communication through websites and social media like Facebook, Ecademy, LinkedIn and Twitter.

If you are going to an event to speak to people one to one, then you can gauge their response to your words in real time through the expression on their faces. Even better, you can edit, revise and enhance what you have to say before you speak to person number two. Once you get involved in newspaper adverts, leaflets and the web you are not only committing yourself in 'print', but you are also committing yourself financially and it can be expensive to reprint leaflets or change websites.

You need to be clear about who you want to speak to and how they like to be communicated with. All of this might not be necessary if you are reselling bungalows to retired people. Get this clear before you start.

What is your offer? What makes you so special?

Now you know who you want to speak to, why would they want to listen? What makes you or what you have to offer so special? Why is your deal the perfect deal to solve all their problems? This is where the essence of you and what you are doing fits perfectly with your potential clients' values, wants and needs.

You need to do all the classic sales things like create your elevator or stadium pitch – your one-minute summary. You also need to get the tone and the language right – it's all about *them*, not *you*. I really do recommend you get advice and check TheSourcersApprentice.com for the latest events or support that I recommend. I wouldn't want to exclude anyone who develops a brilliant course or resource after the book is committed to print! Check out 'Recommended' at ThePropertyMermaid.com.

How can you prove it? Testimonials

What will your answer be if a client asks you: 'What have you done that earns you the right to talk to me?' Can you answer this question?

- Where were you before you started?

- What have you done?

- What have you got now?

- Who have you done it for?

- What did they think of your service?

Get some testimonials (note to self!). Get them in writing. Even better, get them on video too.

Now what I would say here is that, whatever your story, it is your story and it will be one of achievement. I don't think everyone has to be in debt to be successful – it's not a pre-requisite and it's not a competition. If you claim to be a wounded soldier, ex-junkie, alcoholic who was in debt by £100,000 and your partner left you homeless – cold on the streets – this does not automatically make you a good business partner or a success. Sadly, there are plenty of homeless people with similar stories.

The measure of success comes from the distance travelled and the amount of time you took to get there. Again, it is still not a race or a competition – it's about congruency and authenticity. Personally, I don't enjoy describing myself as a single parent, in social housing, unemployed with £100,000 on

STRATEGY

Do you want to Make More Money from Property? A Personal Investment Plan will set you on a clear path to more income

SOURCING

Have you ever thought of retiring early? Do you want to retire in comfort, not worried about bills, but able to live the life of your dreams? Or would you just like more income than than you have now?

TRAINING

Do you think property is a good idea but don't know where to start? Or have you started and want to Make More Money from Property?

the
Property
sourcers
creating your property nest egg

Vicki and her team can help you with
Sourcing . Strategy . Training

For a free 20 minute consultation with Vicki Wusche, author of
"Make More Money from Property"

Email Today:
Hannah@Wusche-Associates.co.uk
or Call:
07795 492001

the Property sourcers

creating your property nest egg

Make More Money From Property

Vicki Wusche

credit cards. That does not tell the story of who I was – even if some might think it makes a better 'story' for the tabloid drama that seems to attract people.

I was a single parent, former university lecturer who understood how money worked and played the credit card companies at their own game by manipulating 0% credit cards and high-rate savings accounts to my own advantage. I first went on a three-day property course in February 2008 and by the first bank holiday in May I had my area defined and I was connecting with estate agents, viewing properties and putting in offers for buy-to-let properties that I was going to fund with a cash pot created through a family joint venture partnership.

16 months after my first completion, I was buying on average 1–2 properties per month for a year; I had a sourcing business and was just about to write my first book. I had enough personal cashflow that I didn't have to work. Tell your story your way, half full or half empty – it's all about the distance travelled and what you have learnt on the journey.

In 2011, I was fortunate enough to work with Blair Singer and with his help developed the following answer…

Over the last two years, during a period of financial crisis, I have helped over 30 clients increase their financial security by £750,000 by uncovering and refining their personal investment strategies and building cashflowing property portfolios for them while creating my own financial security.

What do you like doing (speaking, writing or are you a 'background' person)?

This is back to knowing yourself and being in your flow. I know a number of property investors who are great with the numbers and doing the deals, but they are just not that fond of speaking to strangers or to groups. They do well because they have found people who they can partner with that complement them. Similarly, if you are all talk and no action or research, then you need a 'numbers and detail' person to make sure that things get done.

Other products

This is both a potential revenue stream and a form of marketing, but is it
an area that you want to get into? I think the answer is yes. Over the years,
I have worked with some great internet marketeers and website/online
marketing geniuses. I think that the best thing I can say at this point is before
you go online understand why you want to do it.

I regularly speak about 'making more money from your property knowledge'
and in fact that is the underlying premise of this book... Start a sourcing
business and leverage your knowledge and so make even more money from
your property knowledge.

Well, once you have got to grips with running this model successfully, then
you can start to think about other ways to make even more money from your
property knowledge. Have you thought of packaging up your knowledge and
experience in some form and selling it to other people?

There are lots of easy products that you can create to increase your exposure
to your market, including e-books about key areas of your experience,
websites/blogs and even videos. For example, what were you before you
became a property business owner? Do you have transferable knowledge
you could share? I know some good friends in property who offer a service
to investors that saves them money on a refurbishment and can even reduce
the purchase price. Could you do that? Could you write a book or hold a mini
workshop?

Basically, everyone wants information – and a lot of people want to know
how to make money, or rather more money. What do you know that can help
people? You can think of your knowledge in two ways: as a free resource
to your potential clients (investors or home sellers) that will help them and
start to build trust so they come to you as their first point of call; or you can
sell your knowledge as a product. Now I am going to be brief here because
otherwise a small minority of you (having read a whole book about setting
up a sourcing business and thinking it was a good idea) will get caught in the

glare of the 'shiny' new idea (I have been there myself) and now be thinking about lots of online products – STOP!

The property sourcing business comes first – just bear in mind that, when the time is right, you can then repurpose your information and create lots of other products and services that can help your clients or create additional revenue streams. A word of warning – writing books seriously reduces your cashflow as you stop focusing on the number of deals you are doing!

Building the business with outside help – the challenge of the joint venture

I think that joint ventures are more of a challenge for two reasons: money and people. Either one is fine but put the two together and it becomes complicated because humans bring emotion and life with them. Emotion and life do not impact on the banks or credit card lenders (although we could debate that – think 2007/8!)

If you change the thought of 'joint venture' into the concept of a 'property sourcing business', then the complications are largely removed. This is because you are either project managing the purchase of a property for someone in return for cash, which often equates to over three years rent share, or you can use their money to fund a deal – again for a fee. It is a business arrangement, which is also what a joint venture should be – it's just that some people forget to cover the detail of the agreement upfront!

Joint ventures need to be about business – a cold hard fact. What is going to be used/borrowed, for what purpose, for how long and at what cost? Then who will do what, where do the responsibilities lie? In a way, just like my sourcing contract, the joint venture document needs to explain the process that will happen to the money, which person has what role, time frames, consequences and ROI.

I prefer to think of joint ventures in a wider context of using other people's money; that way I am not limited to thinking about individuals or angel investors. Everyone is 'other people' so there are lots of sources of money – you just need to be clear on what you are going to do with it and how the owner of the cash will benefit financially.

I feel that this is an advance strategy because it takes us away from the simple repeatable sourcing business model. If you are working with someone who does not want to be an investor themselves, then the cash would be used for flipping or accelerated remortgages and that is a more risky strategy. It involves agreeing to borrow money (with penalties) for a set period in the hope that all things will stay the same while you renovate and refurbish a property in order to meet some predetermined valuation!?!

The point is that borrowing cash from individuals over relatively short periods of time based on future valuations is risky. Why not look more widely at other people's money and see how you can make it work for you? It may be on a slightly slower timescale – but certainly a safer one.

Chapter 11

So, to summarise the whole book...

If you have the mindset of a property business owner, understand how money works and run a replicable cashflow investment model, then it is just a matter of time before you have all the income you need.

In the sentence above the most important words are 'mindset of a property business owner' because if you have that, then you are guaranteed to get the rest – you simply can't fail.

This book is all about the journey I have taken to become a property business owner, but it is not me or my journey that's important – it's what you recognise, feel and even know is relevant to you and what *you* want in life that is most important. In Chapter 1, I refer to 'active responsibility' as being my personal philosophy; in fact, it is the deciding factor in your success.

When you understand and apply 'active personal responsibility' to everything you do, then you will:

- Be clear on what you want to achieve and 'constantly' monitor your performance against your goals;

- Understand how to leverage the relative value of money and identify massive ROI in every deal you do;

- Understand that when you face a challenge it is simply a lesson; you will have the skills to think logically about it, work out the message and then take appropriate action; and

- Be aware of how you spend your time, and value and enjoy every moment because you are monitoring your actions against your goals – which are written down and shared with your coach.

It sounds easy and really it is. What will determine how long it takes you to reach this state of business entrepreneurship is your level of resistance.

You might 'get' these concepts straight away; you might have to put more research or time into understanding the money markets, the maths or the practicalities of finding your area. However long it takes, you will be determined by your willingness to change your approach towards money and helping other people.

By now you will understand that by leveraging your financial resources first, you will be in a far better place to help those around you – it's the difference between thinking like a lottery winner and recognising that you need to put your own mask on first!

Remember that everything you have or do in your life now, is a result of decisions you have or have not taken in the past. Your decisions or lack of them are based on your values, the subconscious filters that you apply and the clarity of your focus. So if you are happy with your life – fantastic – you did that; if you are dissatisfied in anyway whatsoever with your life – then you did that too. This is such an empowering thought – it means you have complete control over the outcome of your life. You can design it, build it, have it and live it. What you do today will change what you can do forever.

Remember, you have a choice – you can go down one of two paths: you can create a future life based on what you don't have in life right now – seeing only the gaps; or you can choose to create a life that is grateful for everything you have and focused on creating even more wealth, health and happiness. Which do you want?

'Who is going to support you?' is a question I haven't asked explicitly. I have talked about my coaches and the mentors that I read, observe or follow. I suggest that if you can see someone who has a life similar to your dream, then think about what values they might have, what they are focused on and what strategies they use, so why reinvent the wheel when standing on the shoulders of giants is much easier? Who is going to be your guide and hold you accountable to a higher level?

You are now able to:

- Understand what you think and how past experiences have shaped you;

- Recognise the little voices that want to help, but might not be relevant anymore;

- Eliminate any limiting beliefs and adopt more empowering values and filters;

- Recognise the power of connecting with your whole mind; and

- Take responsibility for your decisions and their outcomes, good or bad, noting the lessons and adjusting your course as you need to, to stay on the right path.

You are now able to master all the technical skills you need to apply to your business model by:

- Identifying your personal point of financial equilibrium to get your income and expenses in balance;

- Calculating the value of your time and therefore know what strategies are worth your attention and which are a costly distraction;

- Leveraging your resources and use other people's money;

- Giving the lenders what they want and build a financial relationship on your own terms; and

- Knowing what is important to watch in the world economy and make informed decisions about longer-term financial strategies.

So all that is left of course... is to take action!

You are a business owner

You are taking this knowledge and understanding and applying it to your own circumstances. You are creating your own repeatable and replicable model of property sourcing. You have identified where your skills and experience lie and what your knowledge and passion is about. You know who you can go to for coaching, support and accountability.

You are following these steps to success, financial security and a fulfilling life:

1. Identifying **why** you want to invest in property, what you expect to get out of it, what the business will look like, how much you will earn (do the maths) and how you will earn your cashflow.
2. Getting financially **educated**; you have read Kiyosaki's *Rich Dad Poor Dad* and *Rich Dad's Conspiracy of the Rich: The 8 New Rules of Money*.
3. Expanding your **network** by looking at who you mix with – what groups you attend or join, like Ecademy (I can send you a trial invitation if you like).
4. Choosing the right **strategy** in the knowledge that the other strategies can be used if need be.
5. Remembering the value of your **time**! Understanding what you want to achieve financially and giving yourself the best possible chance of achieving it. Becoming your own client and making sure that you earn a decent income for your time.
6. **Leveraging** other people's money and other people's time. Understanding the relative cost of money and ROI and explaining the opportunity to potential clients.
7. Understanding what you have to **offer** your clients, what your service is and why they should buy from, sell or rent to you and not someone else.
8. Building the right **team** and mastering your leadership skills.

In Section 3, I have explained, step by step, my replicable model of identifying and offering cashflowing properties to clients who have money or equity sitting in low returning vehicles and who want to make better use of their money.

I am creating a series of mini video blogs to take you through the whole process. Working with Loran, my business partner, I will explain each step and then record her experience and challenges as they arise. The combination of describing, applying and reflecting on each step will give you a unique 'fly on the wall' experience. These are available through TheSourcersApprentice.com.

I know and really believe you can increase the money you earn from your property knowledge. I know you can build a better business. I also know that you will face challenges; otherwise you would not be reading this book. I am happy to support those of you who are serious about driving your business forward.

Together, Loran and I have created Wealth^N. Wealth to the Nth degree combines my investment and business model and multiplies it with Loran's advanced coaching skills to hold you accountable on a level you will not have experienced before. This is an application-only programme as we only achieve 100% success.

Whatever you do from now on is of course up to you – you are the creator of your future. Your life when you are 40, 50, 60, 70 and beyond is being created right now – what is your life going to be like? I'll see you scuba diving in the warm water coral reefs somewhere... ☺

Glossary

Asset: an investment that generates a profit – puts cash in your pocket.

AST: an assured shorthold tenancy agreement – a contract between landlord and tenant explaining responsibilities and duties. Usually written for period of six months though can be longer.

B2L or buy to let: the process of buying a property with the intention of renting it to a third party to make a profit from the rent paid.

BMV (below market value): a specific term meaning a strategy that relies on getting a specific property valuation at a point in the future to enable all capital invested in a purchase to be recouped or released.

Bridging finance: a specific source of secured funding that some investors use to fund certain deals that require a quicker remortgage or are not eligible for mortgaging. This is an expensive source of funding and requires specialist advice.

EPC (energy performance certificate): legal requirement on any property being sold or rented.

ERC (early redemption charge): liable if you redeem a mortgage sooner than an agreed date.

HMO (house of multiple occupancy): often student housing or professional multi-lets. Each council will have their own area-specific requirements, but broadly any property over three storeys high with three or more unrelated occupants will be eligible for licensing.

Joint venture: usually refers to a business agreement to access someone else's cash for investment purposes – could be similar to a private form of bridging finance though often less expensive.

Lease option: a specific strategy aiming to control rather than own an asset or property. Popular in land and commercial deals – it has become popularised in the UK and like other more 'unusual' schemes it is under the watchful eye of the Financial Standards Authority. Eventually this will become a licensable strategy.

Leverage: the concept of taking a resource and multiplying the effect it can have – an example is buying a property using a mortgage where, for a fee, a lender supplies some of the capital required – another example is outsourcing where a person supplies time in return for a fee.

Liability: an investment or purchase that costs you money on a monthly basis – takes money from your pocket.

No money down (NMD): a strategy popular in 2008 to early 2010 where through various schemes 'deal makers' sought to offer properties for sale for a fee (to them) but no cash was actually required to purchase the house. The properties were then highly leveraged and often low or negative rent producing.

No money left in: a strategy that we all aspire to – the aim to buy a property and enhance its value so that at the point of remortgage you are able to release all the initial capital that you invested – leaving none of your own money in the deal.

ROI (return on investment): a useful tool to compare the benefit of investing in one specific asset compared to another, or compared to leaving funds in the bank.

ROTI (return on time invested): a tool to identify the real profit in a specific action, by including the cost of your time to ensure that a deal or purchase actually completes.

Strategy: this can be a way to describe the type of properties you buy, for example buy to let usually means houses let on an AST or HMOs. It can also describe the type of investment strategy being used, for example lease options, NMD or joint venture.

Yield: a figure to describe the average return possible based on gross figures.

Bibliography

Publications

Canfield, J. (et al) (2009) *Chicken Soup for the Entrepreneur's Soul*, Health Communications.

Dass, S. (2010) *Traders, Guns and Money: Knowns and Unknowns in the Dazzling World of Derivatives*, FT/Prentice Hall.

Evans, T. (2010) *Flavours of Thought: Recipes for fresh thinking*, CompletelyNovel.com.

Evans, T. (2011) *The Art and Science of Light Bulb Moments*, O Books.

Hill, N. (1960) *Think and Grow Rich*, Highroads.

Howard, C. (2005) *Turning Passions Into Profits*, John Wiley & Sons.

Howard, C. (2010) *Instant Wealth – Wake up Rich!*, John Wiley & Sons.

Kiyosaki, R. (2002) *Rich Dad Poor Dad*, Time Warner.

Kiyosaki, R. (2009) *Rich Dad's Conspiracy of The Rich: The 8 New Rules of Money*, Hachette.

Kiyosaki, R. (2011) *An Unfair Advantage: The Power of Financial Education*, Plata Publishing.

Maxwell, J. C. (1998) *The 21 Irrefutable Laws of Leadership*, Thomas Nelson.

Metcalf, F. (2003) *Buddha in your Backpack*, Ulysses Press.

Morris, C. R. (2009) *Two Trillion Dollar Meltdown: Easy Money, High Rollers, and the Great Credit Crash*, PublicAffairs.

Olson, J. (2005) *The Slight Edge*, Momentum Media.

Power, P. (2009) *Know Me, Like Me, Follow Me: What Online Social Networking Means for You and Your Business*, Headline Business Plus.

Rajan, R. G. (2011) *Fault Lines: How Hidden Fractures Still Threaten the World Economy*, Princeton University Press.

Redfield, J. (1994) *The Celestine Prophecy*, Bantam.

Rohn, J. (1993) *The Art of Exceptional Living* [Audiobook], Nightingale Conant.

Singer, B. (2008) *Little Voice Mastery*, Xcel Holdings.

Trump, D. and Kiyosaki, R. (2006) *Why We Want You to Be Rich*, Rich Press.

Upton, D. (2009) *Create Your Desires and Fulfill Your Dreams*, UKUnpublished.

Weerasinghe, R. Dr (2011) *Turning Point*, Ecademy Press.

Wusche, V. (2010) *Using Other People's Money: How to Invest in Property*, Vizzi Publishing.

_____

e-books

Evans, T. (2011) *Goals of Learning: A simple guide to a wonder-full life*, available from TheSourcersApprentice.com

Wusche, V. (2011) *Managing Your Credit Cards, Scores and Reports*, available from TheSourcersApprentice.com

Moving forward

Programmes, products and services

It is my mission to inspire and educate people to identify and leverage their previously untapped personal resources, creating generations of financially secure business owners and property investors – that turn our economy back from recession.

I will continue to create a variety of products, services and events to this end.

You will find many free resources on my websites, including a free newsletter focused on financial news, property investment and wealth creation.

Visit

ThePropertyMermaid.Com

and

TheSourcersApprentice.com

Vicki Wusche

Since 1994 Vicki has shared her knowledge and understanding of all things entrepreneurial, wealth and personal development. She has trained or spoken in front of thousands of people across the UK.

During her time working at a high level to influence education policy and teaching, Vicki worked with inspirational entrepreneurs on the cutting edge of a new media revolution while at the same time supporting some of the most deprived people in London through her work as director for two charitable organisations focused on regeneration, housing, refugees and employment and re-inspiring young people.

Throughout her time working in education, and more recently in property investment and wealth creation, Vicki has constantly studied both formally and informally the great minds, concepts and strategies vital to business success. This has led to a Masters Degree, a Diploma in Higher Education, and a Master NLP qualification to mention a few.

In 2006 she was made redundant and decided to step out as a full-time consultant, after working on a freelance basis for the last year. This presented its own challenge and led her again to immerse herself in self-development, which she now points to as the reason for her success.

During 2007 Vicki's attitude towards money changed dramatically as she recognised the power of leverage, the value of her time and how to maximise the return on her investments. Armed with this new understanding in 2008, what seemed an easy process to learn the mechanics of property investing was again an interesting experience as challenge after challenge presented itself as she identified and 'tried' to buy investment properties.

January 2009 saw a dramatic turning point as Vicki recognised she either was going to make a success of property investing or find a job stacking shelves! The next 12 months saw her buy on average 1–2 properties per month and start her sourcing business. By 2010 Vicki's desire to share her knowledge and understanding of property investing and using other people's money led her to publish her first book.

Throughout everything she has done in employment or her entrepreneurial endeavours, the driving force behind Vicki is her family and her desire to help others maximise the resources they have, whether they are mental, emotional, financial or physical.

Now combining all her skills and experience with an ability to translate complex concepts with passion, into to every day practicalities, Vicki is focused on building property portfolios for clients that have access to financial resources. Her clients recognise that this is a once in a generation opportunity to build long-lasting financial security for their families and to secure and leverage their hard-earned wages before inflation erodes them, but lack the time to take advantage – that's where Vicki's experience and service comes in to play.

Together with her business partners, Vicki offers a range of support for those looking to build their own business in property or expand their commercial businesses.

The Property Sourcers

The key to your property investment nest egg

Do you want to get paid to live in your home?

Do you want 14% interest on your money guaranteed?*

For those of you that are asset or equity rich, but time poor, this is your opportunity to build wealth! After experiencing a personalised strategy session, your financial and investment action plan will be clearly defined. Depending on your circumstances, personal choice and financial situation we can take the hard work out of investing for you. We will produce and fully micro-manage an investment portfolio strategy on your behalf which will allow you to reap the benefits and financial rewards without the effort!

Since 2009 Vicki has been using her experience and knowledge of the property market to build cashflowing property portfolios for bespoke clients.

Offering returns on investment of over 10%*, the properties that Vicki sources are identified to generate cashflow and create financial security for clients, leaving them to focus on their lives.

During the last 12 months Vicki has been able to secure access to a unique investment opportunity and together with her contractors can now also provide guaranteed high returns of 14-25%* for specific clients that meet the investment criteria. Investment opportunities start as low as £30,000* per property and average £55,000* per property.

The process will start with a personalised strategy session. During two and a half hours Vicki works personally with you to help you recognise the pros and cons of property investment, recognise your personal investment goals and identify a clear investment strategy. While the majority of clients (over 80%)

---

*Interest rates, ROIs and guarantees are property specific and subject to your personal financial circumstances.

go on to invest with Vicki, this is not a sales pitch. You will leave with a clear investment strategy that enables you to make the right investment choices, at the right time, for you.

With the development of The Property Sourcers, Vicki and Loran can now work with a discrete group of cash-rich investors offering a hands-free process designed to balance the investors' needs for security and flexibility with a busy life. They aim to place just 20 of these unique properties over the next 12 months with a further 30 traditional buy-to-let properties.

This service is not for everyone, clients will need to pass credit checks, have a provable income and have access to financial resources. Professional advice will be provided throughout the process through a team of experts in the property, tax and financial world. With lending criteria becoming increasingly challenging, please contact Vicki and her team to arrange a free, no-obligation call to assess whether this programme suits your needs and circumstances and takes away your worries and concerns, then book your strategy session to determine your Readiness to Invest.

For further information on this service visit The PropertySourcers.com or email Hannah at info@ThePropertySourcers.co.uk to arrange your personalised 'Ready to Invest' strategy session.

The Sourcers Apprentice

Do you want to start your own property business?

Did you enjoy reading this book and want to implement it straight away? Do you feel that you still want even more detail and a step-by-step process to creating your cashflowing sourcing business?

Vicki Wusche and Loran Northey

Could you be making even more money from your property knowledge?

Vicki recognises that even though she explains the importance of leverage and return on time, some people still want to create their own property investment business – like she has. They have a passion for property and enjoy the houses, the numbers, the challenges and the excitement.

Based on her education background and experience, Vicki knows that the next best thing to immersing yourself in a live programme is watching and copying those steps in real time through video and audio programmes.

The Sourcers Apprentice programme is an audio/video and workbook solution to help you rapidly build a successful property investment business. Join us in this informative, in-depth and incredibly valuable multi-learning tool, which takes you from the fundamental inspiration stage right through on a step-by-step learning process to the successful creation of your own personalised business model. Providing you with all the documents, research tools, what and what not to dos, plus hand-holding instructional information to enable you to become a highly effective, cash flowing and profitable property sourcer.

The videos and audios enable people to use the learning outlined in this book and take it to another level. Implementing the steps that Vicki and Loran demonstrate and describe, you can learn the theory, watch as Loran implements the steps Vicki teaches and then hear her reflect on the experience uncovering new insights.

For further information please visit TheSourcersApprentice.com.